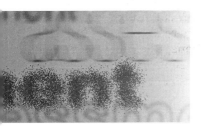

Contents

Introduction
to the
third edition

Good teaching is about motivating and helping children to learn. Teachers typically treat assessment as a necessary chore rather than as an intrinsic part of this process: the idea of going into teaching because of a love of assessment would seem bizarre. This is hardly surprising when so much of current national assessment appears to be less to do with individual achievement than with monitoring school performance. What we seek to do in this book is to show how teacher assessment is central to effective learning and to evaluate the high-profile uses of external assessment for selection and for monitoring standards.

Why do teachers need to know about assessment? At one level the answer is obvious enough: national assessment tests and public examinations are part of the education system in the UK. Standardised tests may be used in a screening programme to identify children who need special provision of one sort or another; and also for diagnosis of individual pupil's strengths and weaknesses. Tests and examinations are used for selection (to secondary school in some cases, or to higher education), for certification and for reporting progress to parents. Results of public examinations and national assessment are used to monitor the performance of the education system and as an accountability measure for schools and LEAs. Teachers' own assessments are used for record-keeping, to monitor their teaching and – most importantly – to support pupil learning: assessment of this more informal kind is a crucial part of teachers' work, fitting into the teaching–learning cycle.

The list of uses of assessment outlined in the paragraph above could, of course, be expanded, but the main uses are there.

In the previous edition of this book we divided these into *managerial* or *professional* categories. By **professional**, we mean that assessment primarily helps the teacher in the process of educating the pupil, while **managerial** means using test and assessment results to help manage the education system. Screening and diagnosis can be identified as mainly managerial uses, while record-keeping and feedback on performance can operate at both levels. It is important to remember that if the main beneficiary of assessment is the learner, then professional uses are the more important. Certification and selection are artefacts of our social and educational system; they, and the assessments which support them, are **not** central to the teaching and learning of the individual.

An alternative categorisation is *assessment of learning* or *assessment for learning*. Assessment **of** learning can be equated with managerial purposes and is essentially summative: it takes place at the end of a period of teaching/schooling and the results or information produced are used outside the classroom. Assessment **for** learning, by contrast, can be equated with professional purposes and is essentially formative: it takes place at any time but is more useful during a period of teaching; the information produced is used by the teacher in the classroom and perhaps by other teachers in the school. (Assessment of learning may also mean assessment of the pupils' understanding and mental processes, rather than – as used here – assessment of their performance.) We will be using assessment *of* and *for* learning in this book because, since we wrote the 1993 edition, we and others working in the field have become ever more aware of the key role that assessment has to play in learning.

Our emphasis is on primary and secondary school assessment in England, Wales and Northern Ireland – with glances towards Scotland, where more constructive solutions often seem to have been found. We have not attempted to provide a 'how to' manual, nor a highly technical account of assessment issues. For those who require these, we refer to good recent accounts.

We have organised and re-written the book to reflect the trends in assessment and the specific interests of teachers. We begin with what, historically, has been the central role of testing: to raise standards and to provide fairer ways of selection. In chapter 2 we move to classroom assessment, which we argue is critical to effective learning: this chapter raises the issue of the learning processes we want for our students, and whether our classroom assessments and national tests really encourage these. Chapter 3 looks at what has recently become the main use of external, standardised assessment: its use to monitor and compare the performance of schools, local education authorities and even nations. We review the issues around performance tables, the move to 'value-added' measures as an alternative, and the use of comparability studies to monitor standards over time and across nations. In chapters 4 and 5 we provide a more technical treatment of some of the issues already raised: validity and reliability, criterion- and norm-referencing, and fairness and bias in testing.

Chapter 6 deals with the main assessment issues facing primary school teachers and pupils, including the effects of national curriculum assessment. Chapter 7 parallels this in addressing assessment issues for secondary teachers and pupils. This includes the transfer to secondary school, Key Stage 3 testing and examinations at 16 and 18. Chapter 8 looks at some of the assessment issues around vocational qualifications, as they become increasingly available in schools and colleges.

We conclude with some proposals as to how current assessment policies could be modified and improved. We hope that we have provided readers with ways of thinking about assessment that will enable them to evaluate both present and future assessment policy.

Gordon Stobart and Caroline Gipps

Acknowledgements

This book draws on many sources, as well as our own research. *Caroline Gipps* would like to thank the ESRC for funding of the National Assessment in Primary Schools and the Teacher Feedback to Young Children projects, and her colleagues in those studies: Pat Tunstall, Margaret Brown, Bet McCallum, Shelley McAlister, Brenda Taggart, and also Patricia Murphy. Some of these chapters draw on previously published work, and thanks are due to the publishers for their permission:

Falmer Press: *Beyond Testing: Towards a theory of educational assessment*, by Gipps, C. (1994)

Open University Press: *Intuition or Evidence?*, by Gipps, C, Brown, M., McCallum, B. and McAlister, S. (1995)

Open University Press: *A Fair Test?*, by Gipps, C. and Murphy, P. (1994)

Gordon Stobart writes here in a personal capacity. He would like to thank Steve Edwards for his contributions on special educational needs and his constructive comments on early drafts, and Marie Adams for her good-humoured editing.

We should both like to acknowledge the role of the BERA Policy Task Group on Assessment for valuable discussions, and in particular the use of the article by Harlen, W., Gipps, C., Broadfoot, P. and Nuttall, D. published in 1992 and updated by Mary James, 'Assessment and the Improvement of Education', *The Curriculum Journal*, 3, 3, 215-230.

Finally, drawing together all this material has been a considerable technical task and we should like to thank Kate Myronidis for her calm, competent and cheerful typing, faxing and disk conversion; Lisa Picknell for her work on the tables and on harmonising our various PC systems; and Laura Stobart for help with references and with Chapter 8.

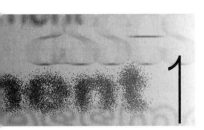

Assessment of learning: standards and selection

Gillian Sutherland (1996) argues that three uses of assessment have dominated its history in Britain so far: as a device for raising standards, as a device for measuring deviation or abnormality, and as a device for securing equitable treatment. This chapter looks at these uses, taking a historical perspective in order to make sense of some of the assumptions with which we currently operate.

Raising standards: a brief history

While there has been a long history of oral and practical examinations associated with universities and trade guilds, formal written examinations were not widely used at Cambridge and Oxford until the eighteenth century. One of the first of these was the product of concern at St John's College at the standards of performance of its students, who from 1765 had to sit twice-yearly domestic tests (Sutherland 1996). There was also widespread abuse of the oral examination, exemplified in Vicessimus Knox's outraged account in 1778 of the Oxford final examinations:

> ❝As neither the officer, nor anyone else, usually enters the room (for it is considered very ungenteel), the examiners (usually three MAs of the candidate's own choice) usually converse on the last drinking bout or on horses or read the newspaper, or a novel, or divert themselves as well as they can in any manner until the clock strikes eleven, when all parties descend and the 'testimonium' is signed by the masters. ❞
>
> (Broadfoot 1979, p.29)

Broadfoot points out that, in effect, *'four years' residence was the only qualification for a degree – not an inappropriate training for an elite for which the qualifications were almost entirely social'* (op cit).

This mood changed in the nineteenth century and by 1852 the Royal Commissioners investigating the affairs of Oxford University commented: *'to render a system of examination effectual it is indispensable that there should be a danger of rejection for inferior candidates, honourable distinctions and substantial rewards for the able and diligent'* (Carr-Saunders and Wilson 1933, p.309). This comment serves as a useful introduction to the theme of formal assessment being used to ensure *fairness* in judging the performance of students and institutions. It is a theme to which we return in chapter 5.

Professional qualifying examinations

Formal qualifying examinations for the professions began in Britain in the early nineteenth century. It was the medical profession which, in 1815, first instituted qualifying examinations; these examinations were to determine competence and therefore limited access to membership of the profession (Broadfoot 1979). Written examinations for solicitors came in 1835 and for accountants in 1890.

Why was it necessary for the professions to institute these qualifying examinations? Part of the answer lay in the changing needs and structure of society. But, as we shall see later in this chapter, they were also introduced as a check on standards. Before the nineteenth century, England was a society in which social status and occupation were linked and determined largely by birth. Access to the professions was determined by family history and patronage, rather than by academic achievement or ability. As Eggleston (1984) points out, the celibate priesthood was virtually the only 'open' career opportunity in those times.

Soon after the beginning of the nineteenth century this static picture began to change. As the industrial capitalist economy flourished, there was an increasing need for trained, middle-class workers. This need could not be satisfied by the traditional methods of nomination and patronage alone. The economy required, in particular, more individuals in the professions and in managerial positions. Society therefore needed to encourage a wider range of individuals to take on these roles. The expanding middle classes realised that education was a means of acquiring social status, and they could see that it was in their children's interests to encourage them to aim for the professions. This was the first time that upward mobility became a practical proposition on a wide scale. Of course, there had to be some way of selecting those who were deemed suitable for training, as well as certificating those who were deemed to be competent. Thus it became necessary for the professions to control access and membership through examination. The examination was also seen as an important part of professionalisation.

School examinations

As the numbers seeking higher education increased, so did the provision of secondary education. Some of this was of doubtful quality, particularly the proprietary boarding school – often the speculative venture of a joint stock company (Sutherland 1990). Anxiety about the standards of provision led to the creation of local examination boards connected to Oxford, Cambridge and London universities. It was still possible to buy your way into university, but before this, entry had been determined *solely* by family background. In 1855 the Civil Service entry examinations were introduced in order to select candidates for the rapidly expanding civil service. Though the aim was to *broaden* access, it was still almost exclusively those who had received an appropriate fee-paying education who were able to pass these examinations (Eggleston, *op cit*).

Before 1917 there was a range of competing school-leaving examinations, some of which were linked to particular professions and universities, but in 1917 formal examining at the end of secondary schooling was rationalised when the School Certificate was established. The School Certificate provided a standard school-leaving and university entrance qualification (Broadfoot, *op cit*), which was necessary because of the increasing numbers completing secondary schooling. To obtain the School Certificate required a pass in five or more academic subjects, with music and manual subjects being optional. The reason why the formal written examination of academic subjects was seen to be so important was that most of the early qualifying examinations for entrance to the professions were written theoretical tests: because they were associated with high-status professions, this type of examination also became invested with high status. This then became the model for university entrance and School Certificate examinations.

The point here is that these examinations did *not* develop in a vacuum: examinations developed in response to the particular needs and requirements of the time, and standards were a key theme.

RAISING STANDARDS IN ELEMENTARY SCHOOLS
Just as the middle classes were pressing for more secondary education, so too came pressure for elementary education for the working classes. The government began offering grants in 1833 and expenditure rose dramatically as demand for them increased. This was accompanied by controversy about what was happening in the schools, with claims that teachers were concentrating on the most able children and neglecting the others. The result of all this was the notorious *payment by results* scheme introduced in the 1862 Revised Code of Robert Lowe. Under this scheme the bulk of funding depended on the annual performance of each child in examinations in reading, writing and arithmetic. The examination 'standards' were age-related and no child was allowed to sit the examination at the same standard twice. The scheme was pushed through despite the opposition of the inspectorate – who had to implement it – and it stayed in place for the next thirty years.

Lowe maintained his intention was to raise standards, '*by which he meant that teachers should be driven by threats of financial penalty to bring the largest possible number of children up to a minimum level of attainment*' (Sutherland 1996, p.11). He defended the scheme, and the deployment of inspectors to operate it, in terms that resonate with us in the current age of pupil-led and 'outcomes related' funding and the inspection processes of the 1990s:

> ❝*What is the object of inspection? Is it simply to make things pleasant, give the schools as much as can be got out of the public purse, independent of their efficiency. . . . Are you for efficiency or subsidy? Is a school to be relieved because it is bad and therefore poor, or because it is a good school, and therefore efficient and in good circumstances?* ❞
> (*Hansard's Parliamentary Debates, 13.2.1862, 205* – cited in Sutherland 1996)

As critics had predicted, the scheme dramatically reduced government expenditure on elementary schools for the next eight years. Whether standards improved was impossible to judge, particularly as the relationship between inspectors and schools soured. The inspectors' role, formerly one of advice and support, was aptly described by one headmaster as '*to criticise and fine*' (*op cit*).

What this historical episode clearly shows is that using assessment to raise standards may have unintended consequences, a theme to which we return in later chapters. Not only did the scheme eventually collapse under its own bureaucratic weight, it also produced some of the worst examples of 'teaching to the test'. Edward Holmes, a former Senior Inspector, reflected:

> ❝*When inspectors ceased to examine (in the stricter sense of the word) they realised what infinite mischief the yearly examination had done. The children, the majority of whom were examined in reading and dictation out of their own reading books . . . were drilled in the contents of those books until they knew them almost by heart. In arithmetic they worked abstract sums in obedience to formal rules, day after day, month after month. . . . They learned a few lines of poetry by heart, and committed all the 'meanings and illusions' to memory. . . . In geography, history and grammar they were the victims of unintelligent oral cram, which they were compelled, under pains and penalties, to take in and retain until the examination day was over. . . . Not a thought was given, except in a small minority of the schools, to the real training of the child, to the fostering of his mental (and other) growth. To get him through the yearly examination by hook or by crook was the one concern of the teacher.* ❞
> (Holmes 1911, pp.107–8)

While our current use of assessment to monitor the standards of pupil and school performance may avoid the excesses of Lowe's scheme, we still need to reflect on our current approaches to see whether these too might be distorting the 'real training' of pupils. It also raises the important question of the role of tests in raising standards.

Can testing raise standards?

The introduction of the national curriculum and assessment was described as a proven and acceptable way of raising standards (DES 1987a). But there is little *evidence* that the introduction of mandated testing raises 'standards' short of teaching to the test – and teaching to the test is usually narrowing. However, what we have here is the introduction of mandated testing linked to specific curriculum objectives (initially, the Statements of Attainment; more recently, the Level Descriptions) and a high significance placed on the results.

This is what the Americans call Measurement Driven Instruction, or MDI, involving:

> **❝** *... the use of high-stakes achievement tests to direct the instructional process. The logic of MDI is that when an important consequence of a high stake, such as obtaining a high school diploma or a teaching certificate, is tied to test performance, the content reflected in the test will be incorporated into instruction. The consequence associated with test performance will force an instructional response and the content of the test will 'drive' instruction. The higher the stakes, the greater the impact on instruction.* **❞**
>
> (Airasian 1988)

The perceived benefits of MDI, according to Madaus (1988), are that if the skills are well chosen, with the tests truly measuring them, and the goals of instruction are explicit, then teacher and student efforts are focused on well-defined targets. It also generates clear and uniform standards; easier and more objective accountability at all levels; and has concrete information on how well the schools are doing for the public.

As a result of his work, Madaus framed a number of principles:

PRINCIPLE 1   The power of tests and examinations to affect individuals, institutions, curriculum or instruction is a perceptual phenomenon. If students, teachers or administrators believe that the results of an examination are important, it matters very little whether this is really true or false. The effect is produced by what individuals perceive to be the case.

So what matters is not whether a test *is* high-stakes, but whether participants *believe* it to be high-stakes. This explains the symbolic powers of tests in the mind of policy-makers, particularly in relation to standards. Policy-makers realise the high symbolic value attached to testing: by requiring testing to take place, they can be seen to be tackling the problem of standards.

PRINCIPLE 2   The more any quantitative social indicator is used for social decision-making, the more likely it will be to distort and corrupt the social processes it is intended to monitor.

While testing is seen historically as a relatively objective way of adjusting the system, the negative impact eventually outweighs any benefit, and when test results are used for important social decisions, the changes in the teaching system brought about by such a use can be both substantial and corrupting.

PRINCIPLE 3   If important decisions are presumed to be related to test results, then teachers will teach to the test.

High-stakes testing can indeed focus teaching on to that which is measured by the test. However, it tends to be the scores on the test which rise, and not necessarily that the skill itself improves, so that the teaching is aimed at the test item, and the item format, rather than at the construct or the skill which it intends to measure.

PRINCIPLE 4   In every setting where a high-stakes operates, a tradition of past examinations develops, which eventually *de facto* defines the curriculum.

PRINCIPLE 5   Teachers pay particular attention to the form of the questions on a high-stakes test (for example, short-answer essay, multiple-choice) and adjust their instruction accordingly.

PRINCIPLE 6   When test results are the sole, or even partial, arbiter of future educational or life choices, society tends to treat test results as the major goal of schooling, rather than as a useful but fallible indicator of achievement.

PRINCIPLE 7   A high-stakes test transfers control over the curriculum to the agency which sets or controls the exam.

(Madaus 1988, pp.88–97)

It is important, however, to recognise two points. First, testing can bring about constructive and positive curriculum change. An example of this in

England was the introduction of the GCSE examination at 16, which was designed specifically to counteract the damaging influence of the old O level examination, and to bring in a wider range of student activity, moving away from a narrow, paper and pencil examination mode. Evidence indicates that this indeed is what happened, once teachers got used to the new system (HMI 1989). Second, as we will show in chapter 6, the complex effects of an assessment programme on teachers' practice can be generally positive.

Assessment and selection: intelligence testing

The history of the development and use of intelligence testing, which played so central a role in schooling in the early and mid twentieth century, further illustrates the uses and abuses of testing in this case when used for selection. We look first at the use of intelligence tests for identifying pupils with special educational needs and show how the criterion for selection has moved on from the use of a single score to a complex multi-stage process. We then consider the use of IQ tests, in the guise of the eleven-plus, for selection to secondary school and some of the criticisms they have attracted.

SELECTION FOR SPECIAL EDUCATION

The intelligence test movement developed as a separate strand from examinations. In 1905 Binet, a French psychologist, published the first intelligence test, which was for identifying children with special educational needs. His approach to the development of the test was a practical, even pragmatic, one: test items of an educational nature were chosen for their effectiveness in distinguishing between children who were judged by their teachers to be 'bright' or 'dull' (Wood 1985). These tests would generate a standardised score for each child – an Intelligence Quotient – which has passed into the language as 'IQ score'.

One of the reasons for this interest in IQ testing was that as more and more children were brought into compulsory primary education, there was concern about the increasing numbers of children who were thought to be subnormal and therefore ineducable. Binet's test was an ideal tool for identifying 'feeble-minded' children, and other tests were later developed by English psychologists – notably Cyril Burt and Charles Spearman as well as by Godfrey Thomson, later, at Moray House in Scotland.

Cyril Burt himself was installed in 1913 as the first psychologist for the London County Council to help with provision for subnormal children to keep them out of ordinary schools, and he used IQ tests to identify these children. Interestingly, Burt saw the definition of subnormality in administrative terms: *'mental deficiency must be treated as an administrative rather than as a psychological concept'* and *'For immediate practical purposes the only satisfactory definition of mental deficiency is a percentage definition based on the amount of existing accommodation'* (Burt 1921, p.167). As the special schools of London could cater for only 1.5% of the child population, this is where Burt advocated that the cut-off between normal and subnormal performance should be set. Burt found that 1.5% of the population fell below a score equivalent to an IQ of 70 on the Stanford-Binet test (a modification of Binet's original test). So a cut-off of IQ 70 was advocated by Burt, to match the 'subnormal' population with the facilities then available to him. This IQ figure has been widely used as a cut-off point since that time.

The significance of Burt's appointment to the London County Council was that he was not a medical man: his post marked the beginning of the professionalisation of psychology as a discipline, with its own expertise and an aura of scientific respectability (Thomson and Sharp, 1988). These factors were crucial to the acceptance of IQ testing: it was scientific, and therefore 'objective', and the single figure was a marvellous shorthand way of describing children. This simplicity has always been part of the appeal of IQ testing. Furthermore, the theory behind the tests suggested that these measures could be used to predict future academic performance.

Redefining assessment of special educational needs

More recent approaches to the tests with which educational psychologists identify pupils with special educational needs show that a shift in thinking has occurred, reflecting Spearman's injunction (now seventy years old) that *'in truth, "intelligence" has become a mere vocal sound with so many meanings that finally it has none'* (Spearman 1927). The recent publication of the second edition of the British Ability Scales, widely used by psychologists in the assessment of individual children, explicitly abandons the terms *'intelligence'* and *'IQ'*. Significantly, cognitive ability tests (as they are now described) are no longer viewed as a measure of innate capacity or potential. Rather, test scores are seen as *'indicating that, at the present time, the child's cognitive abilities have developed to a particular level relative to other children of the same age and should not be interpreted as indicating an upper limit, or ceiling, of development beyond which the child cannot move'*. Such negative usage of the term *'potential'* is now regarded as unjustified. Indeed, any comprehensive assessment of an individual's abilities and achievements should now reflect a conjunction of information obtained from formal tests of cognitive abilities and *'life information, observations and other test results'*. The 'science' of assessment has moved a long way from the use of tests to identify feeble-minded children.

The assessment of special educational needs has increasingly become the responsibility of those within schools rather than of external specialists . In this regard, recent legislation (notably the 1993 Education Act and the Code of Practice) has been more prescriptive of the role and practice of teachers than anything that preceded it. Extensive demands have been made on schools to develop effective systems for the identification and assessment of the special educational needs of pupils and to set up procedures for recording proposed interventions and reviewing outcomes. Headteachers are formally accountable to their governing bodies for the effective design and implementation of these procedures, and the system is policed by periodic OFSTED inspections as part of a general review of the school's effectiveness. Local education authorities (LEAs) are accountable to the DFEE for ensuring that schools *'pay due regard'* to the Code of Practice, and for the development of effective arrangements for the statutory assessment of individual pupils (more commonly, but incorrectly, known as the *statementing procedure*).

The Code describes five Stages of Assessment of the needs of individual pupils with learning difficulties. At Stage One, it is essentially the responsibility of the class teacher to identify and record needs of individual pupils and develop appropriate in-class arrangements to meet these needs. Stage Two is reached if these arrangements are considered unsuccessful and promotes the role of the school's special educational needs coordinator in supporting the class teacher in the further assessment of need, in developing and reviewing Individual Education Plans and in consulting outside agencies such as the school's educational psychologist or a specialist teaching service. Stage Three is reached when it is felt that the direct involvement of an outside agency in work with the child and their parents is indicated.

These initial stages fall within a school's normal arrangements, the assumption being that the pupil's needs can and should be met from 'resources normally available to the school'. If it is felt that the pupil's needs cannot be met within normal arrangements, then the school can make a proposal to the LEA that the pupil should be made the subject of a statutory assessment (Stage Four) which may or may not lead to the LEA producing a Statement of Special Educational Needs (Stage Five). A Statement usually but not always involves the provision of additional, centrally funded, resources or, less frequently, a recommendation for alternative educational placement, such as a special school.

LEAs and schools are only required to 'pay due regard to' the Code of Practice in developing arrangements to meet the special educational needs of pupils; they are not required in law to follow all its recommendations in every detail. In reality, however, schools and LEAs regard the Code as the template for practice.

The spirit and intention of the Code of Practice are laudable: pupils' needs should be met within Stages One to Three (i.e. normal arrangements), with recourse to statutory assessment only in exceptional cases; effective intervention at these earlier stages preventing the need for more costly interventions at a later date. The effective implementation of the Code's main tenets is, however, something that schools and LEAs may aspire to but rarely attain, given the heavily bureaucratic, costly and time-consuming procedure.

The lesson from this is how we have moved away from confidence in a single test measure, to processes which look at a much fuller picture in arriving at a diagnosis of a pupil's needs.

Selection for secondary education

At the same time as Binet was developing tests to identify pupils who required special education, psychologists had been working on the theory of intelligence – trying to define 'the essence of intelligence'. In 1904, a year before Binet's test appeared, Charles Spearman published a classic paper on general intelligence. Binet and Spearman were critical of each others' work, but the serendipitous timing of developments in the measurement and theory of intelligence gave IQ testing considerable appeal in the eyes of those responsible for the efficient functioning of the state education system (Thomson and Sharp, *op cit*).

As the focus in educational organisation shifted towards coping with the increasing numbers of children staying on into secondary education, so the role of IQ testing shifted from identifying children who were subnormal, to sorting and selecting normal children in the system.

In England, the 1926 Hadow Report on *The Education of the Adolescent* concluded that almost all children were eligible for secondary education, but not the same secondary education: it talked about the equal cultivation of different capacity. At the end of their primary school careers, at 11, children were to be classified by aptitude and to go to secondary grammar schools, secondary modern schools or to remain in senior classes in the primary school. As the report put it: *'all go forward, though along different paths. Selection by differentiation takes the place of selection by elimination'* (Sutherland 1984). Again, the intention was the most efficient use of educational resources and, where those resources were limited, that they be directed towards those children most able to profit from them.

These suggestions were refined in the Spens Report of 1938, which proposed the tripartite division of secondary education into grammar, modern and technical schools. The aim, however, was the same: 'all go forward, though along different paths' and the IQ tests were to play an important role, through the eleven-plus examination, in the process of selecting those children who were deemed capable of benefiting from the academic grammar schools. This classification became the basis of the tripartite provisions of the 1944 Education Act, in which Burt had considerable influence.

From about 1950 there was a reduction in the status of intelligence testing in both the USA and UK. This reflected a growing scepticism about the fallibility of IQ scores. In the USA this was due to the growing awareness that there was a 'cultural bias' in most tests in favour of children from white, Anglo-Saxon backgrounds. In England and Wales it was the realisation that coaching and practice had significant effects on performance in the eleven-plus. On both sides of the Atlantic the importance of social and cultural factors in test performance began to be recognised and appreciated.

In England and Wales the need for selection and classification declined with the gradual move towards comprehensive schooling. IQ tests for normal children, in the guise of verbal reasoning and non-verbal reasoning tests, became largely unnecessary and thus the critique could be accepted without too much inconvenience. Equality of opportunity was now to mean that all would go forward to the same comprehensive secondary school. In practice, pockets of LEA IQ testing continue to this day as the selection method for those grammar schools which remain, particularly in Northern Ireland. Recent moves to increase selection in secondary school transfer have seen a return to this form of testing even within the comprehensive sector as schools vie for the most able pupils.

SOCIOLOGICAL CRITIQUES

Broadfoot (1996a) describes assessment as a device used within developed societies with mass educational provision as a mechanism of social control; as a rational, and justifiable, basis for the allocation of *'unequally desirable social roles'* as individuals are required to demonstrate competence through a certificating procedure based on competition. The use of a justifiable procedure, and the notion of competition in which individuals compete on an apparently equal basis, allows those who are not successful to accept their own failure. IQ testing was a means of social control *'unsurpassed in teaching the doomed majority that their failure was the result of their own inbuilt inadequacy'* (Broadfoot 1979, p.44). The argument is that intelligence testing obscures the perpetuation of class inequalities (a far higher proportion of middle-class children went to grammar schools) because it legitimates them. In other words, it is not that the middle classes are more intelligent, or better able to acquire intelligence, but that it is defined according to their own characteristics or qualities.

Bourdieu and Passeron (1977) argue similarly that the middle classes, unable to perpetuate their status through capital alone at the beginning of this century, were able to fall back on a second line of defence: a school system which, though apparently allowing equal opportunity, was, in fact, geared to the culture of the ruling class and thus allowed them to perpetuate their privileged position by giving them a head start through success in the education system. Thus, we have the notion of 'cultural capital' as opposed to financial or material capital.

The same critique applies to examinations. Just as we have become more critical about simplistic approaches to intelligence, so also the early claim that examinations were fair for all has been challenged, particularly by sociologists. Their critique is that although examinations – in particular, public examinations – are seen as an equaliser in education, the facts belie this argument. The distribution of examination success is persistently linked to social class, gender and race. Again, Bourdieu's argument (very much simplified) is that children from lower social groups are not less intelligent or less academically capable, but that children from middle-class homes are better able to do well at school because of the correspondence of cultural factors between home and school. These factors include the sorts of activities, books and language used at home and at school, attitudes to reading and success at school, etc. Following the IQ argument, the sort of success that counts at school has been determined in terms of middle-class values and experience. Thus, examinations have a legitimating role, in that they allow the ruling classes to legitimate the power and prestige they already have.

Though individual children from non-middle-class families do, of course, obtain academic success, the fact is that in percentage or statistical terms it is a very much lower proportion than from more advantaged homes, and Bourdieu's argument is one way of understanding how this might happen. Here, too, the point to be made is that there is more to be considered than the nature of assessment. The *purpose* of examinations, so the critique goes, is to maintain the social order as well as to select the competent.

Redefining intelligence

In the 1990s the conception of intelligence has changed radically, led by Howard Gardner's work on multiple intelligences:

> **❛**... *students possess different kinds of minds and therefore learn, remember, perform, and understand in different ways. There is ample evidence that some people take a primarily linguistic approach to learning, while others favour a spatial or a quantitative tack. By the same token, some students perform best when asked to manipulate symbols of various sorts, while others are better able to display their understanding through a hands-on demonstration or through interactions with other individuals.*
>
> *I have posited that all human beings are capable of at least seven different ways of knowing the world. . . .***❜**
>
> (Gardner 1991, pp.11–12)

Daniel Goleman's best-selling *Emotional Intelligence* (1995) popularises Gardner's work and emphasises the importance of intuition and emotion in people's lives. The argument advanced is, put simply, that we have in the past conceptualised ability too narrowly in terms of abstract non-verbal and verbal skills.

This supports the message from special education assessment: pupils' abilities and attainments are not measurable in terms of a single dimension and any attempt to reduce performance to a single score is likely to mislead.

In the broader social context, as these examples have shown, we cannot separate the technology of assessment from the values of the educational system and the society in which it operates. Assessment is 'socially embedded' and we can only understand it fully if we take account of the social, economic and political contexts in which it operates (Sutherland 1996).

2 Assessment for learning

Teachers' assessments and learning

It has been known for some time that testing has an effect on teaching, particularly in terms of what is taught. The eleven-plus examination, which determined admission to grammar schools, is a classic example of a test which was of utmost importance for the pupils (defined as 'high-stakes' in chapter 1) and which exerted a stranglehold on the taught curriculum for primary-aged children. The effect of assessment (in its various forms) on *learning*, however, has been unpacked only more recently.

The classic review of the effect of teachers' assessment on pupils was carried out by Crooks (1988). Based on this review, Broadfoot (1996a) summarises how assessment influences learning in four main ways:

1 Assessment provides motivation to learn
- by giving a sense of success in the subject (or demotivation through failure);
- through giving a sense of self-confidence as a learner.

2 Assessment helps students (and teachers) decide what to learn
- by highlighting what is important to learn from what is taught;
- by providing feedback on success so far.

3 Assessment helps students learn how to learn
- by encouraging an active or passive learning style;
- by influencing the choice of learning strategies;
- by inculcating self-monitoring skills;
- by developing the ability to retain and apply knowledge, skills and understanding in different contexts.

4   **Assessment helps students learn to judge the effectiveness of their learning**
   • by evaluating existing learning;
   • by consolidating or transforming existing learning;
   • by reinforcing new learning.

We start by looking at the third of Crooks' list: *Assessment helps students learn how to learn.*

Learning and assessment

Traditional teaching for tests and examinations often encourages rote learning. With rote learning the learners master facts which they can then recall in the test situation. Pupils may become very efficient at this form of memorisation. But facts learnt in this way may be quickly forgotten (how much of your O or A level in Chemistry or Geography can you remember?). Information which is to be retained must either be understood, 'interacted with' and logged in to conceptual maps in the brain, or used repeatedly after learning.

Rote learning, which is essentially passive, can lead to shallow or surface learning. Shallow learning will allow pupils to manipulate formulae or work through detailed exercises, even though they do not understand fundamental principles. This means that pupils may find it hard to use these facts or concepts in other circumstances or contexts, thus limiting the value of their learning.

There is currently a good deal of muddled thinking about the value of rote learning and a return to whole-class teaching. Some of this has been fuelled by a misinterpretation of the success of Pacific Rim countries in international comparisons (see chapter 3). While these countries do use whole-class teaching methods, the approach is far from the stereotype of passive learning. What is seen is a very high rate of interaction between teacher and pupils to make sure there is understanding. This flows from the Confucian tradition of 'repetition as a route to learning':

> ❛*This is an approach to learning which involves memorisation and then constant repetition in order to develop meaning. It is central to learning, for example, Chinese characters, their meaning and how to write them. In its first stage this repetitious learning uses shape, sound, speaking aloud, writing and thinking about the meaning of each of the characters. The second phase is using the meaning and form of the characters to turn them into text. Hence repetition develops meaning. This is not the same as rote learning as it is commonly understood.*

In traditional learning theory the assumption is that rote learning is not meaningful learning, while what is being described in the Confucian tradition is repetitive learning when one already has the meaning. Interestingly, what is described as the Confucian approach to learning and making one's own interpretation of the material at a certain stage of mastery has resonances with constructivist learning theory. The key to both is meaning and understanding. 〉

(Gipps, 'The paradox of the Pacific Rim learner', *TES*, 20 December 1996).

This approach is in many respects nearer to deep learning which involves not only understanding but an intention to understand the material, and requires an active approach to learning. *'Active learning does not mean that learners have to "discover" things for themselves but that they must be actively **thinking for themselves**'* (Harlen and James 1997). Table 2.1 summarises the two approaches.

Table 2.1 Two types of learning (after Entwistle 1992 and Marton and Saljo 1984)

Deep learning approach	Surface or shallow learning approach
An intention to develop personal understanding.	An intention to be able to reproduce content as required.
Active interaction with the content, particularly in relating new ideas to previous knowledge and experience.	Passive acceptance of ideas and information.
Linking ideas together using integrating principles.	Lack of recognition of guiding principles or patterns.
Relating evidence to conclusions.	Focusing learning on assessment requirements.

Of course, some things are most efficiently learned by rote, for example irregular spellings or multiplication tables. Similarly, there is not time to approach all learning in a deep way, so researchers in learning use the notion of *strategic learning*, in which the learner uses a mix of deep and surface approaches. The strategic learner will look at what is required, and for what purpose, and choose the most effective approach.

There is a critical relationship between what is tested, and how it is tested, with what is taught, and how pupils learn. Standardised achievement tests test students' abilities to recall and apply facts learnt routinely; even items which are designed to assess higher level activities often require no more than the ability to recall the appropriate formula and to make substitutions to get the correct answer. Students who conceive of knowledge as collections of facts will use surface-learning strategies that are aimed at successful memorisation. Deep learning in 'good' learners, on the other hand, involves thinking about the meaning of what is being learnt. This notion of purposeful or deep learning clearly has implications for curriculum and pedagogy, but also for assessment. It is a reflection on much of our classroom and examination assessment that even 'deep learners' will opt for last-minute surface-learning approaches as the most effective, since little more than the regurgitation of information is required (Sadler 1989).

Newer models of learning, which see learning as a process of personal knowledge construction and meaning-making, describe a more complex and diverse process than rote learning or absorption of facts. They therefore require assessment to be more diverse and to assess in more depth the structure and quality of students' learning and understanding. While, for example, standardised multiple-choice or short-answer type tests are efficient at sampling the acquisition of specific knowledge, more intense, even interactive assessment such as essays and performance assessments, small group tasks and projects, are needed to get at and encourage a deeper level of learning.

'*Contemporary cognitive psychology has built on the very old idea that things are easier to learn if they make sense*' (Shepard 1991). Isolated facts, if learnt, quickly disappear from the memory because they have no meaning and do not fit into the learner's conceptual map. They cannot be applied, generalised or retrieved. '*Meaning makes learning easier, because the learner knows where to put things in her mental framework, and meaning makes knowledge useful because likely purposes and applications are already part of the understanding*' (Shepard 1992). Aristotle understood this 2300 years ago. He wrote that absorbing knowledge intellectually is not enough to make it usable. To become readily convertible into skilful action it '*must be worked into the living texture of the mind*' (Dixon, in Wolf 1995, p.129).

Newer views of learning indicate why rote learning is difficult to retain in the long term. Learners become more competent, not by learning more facts and skills but by reconfiguring their knowledge. They 'chunk' information to reduce memory load, and develop strategies and models to link sets of information and to enable swift recall. But '*A failure to articulate the relationship between assessment and learning has resulted in a mismatch between the high quality learning described in policy documents as desirable and the poor quality learning that seems likely to result from associated assessment procedures*' (Willis 1992). Although assessment on its own cannot change approaches to learning, we know that assessment is a powerful device to help gear teaching and curriculum. In order to encourage the teaching and development of higher-order skills, thinking processes and problem solving we must use assessment which directly reflects these processes.

Educational assessment

The changes in our understanding of learning, together with developments in assessment, have signalled new conceptions of assessment, with a different underlying purpose. Some commentators refer to this as a *paradigm shift* (Broadfoot 1993; Mislevy 1993; Gipps 1994). An early writer on this theme offered a new definition of what he called *educational measurement*, but we would call *educational assessment*; it:

> 1 deals with the individual's achievement relative to himself rather than to others;
>
> 2 seeks to test for competence rather than for intelligence;
>
> 3 takes place in relatively uncontrolled conditions and so does not produce 'well-behaved' data;
>
> 4 looks for 'best' rather than 'typical' performances;
>
> 5 is most effective when rules and regulations characteristic of standardised testing are relaxed;
>
> 6 embodies a constructive outlook on assessment where the aim is to help rather than sentence the individual.
>
> (Wood 1986, p.194)

Wood's argument is that standardised or psychometric testing, in which individuals are compared with each other, on tightly defined, often artificial, tasks, is of limited use and the business of assessment should be re-thought.

We use the term *educational assessment* to distinguish what is essentially assessment **for** learning (although it may be **of** learning too) from the more psychometric approaches that have dominated much of educational measurement, and which we discuss in later chapters. Educational assessment includes criterion-referenced assessment, which tells us what pupils can do rather than where they are in relation to others, teacher assessment, portfolios, project tasks, coursework and pupil self-assessment. We will outline some of these here, others are dealt with in following chapters.

SELF-ASSESSMENT
Pupil self-assessment was first introduced in Britain with the profiling and Records of Achievement (RoA) movement. In self-assessment pupils evaluate their own work, usually against criteria agreed with the teacher, and will set new targets after reflecting on the assessment. This will generally be carried out alongside other assessment activity. The aim of this approach to assessment is not only to encourage pupils to become independent learners, but also to develop *metacognitive* strategies.

Metacognition is the process of being aware of one's own learning: good learners monitor their learning and thinking processes through self-monitoring (or self-regulated learning). '*When students are engaged in evaluating their own work, they are thinking about what they have learnt and how they learn. They are consequently more aware of their thinking and learning processes which encourages a deep, as opposed to a surface, approach to learning. . . . the psychological processes of metacognition map on to student self-evaluation*' (Klenowski 1996, pp.3–4). It also focuses the pupil's evaluation on his or her *own* performance rather than in comparison with others, which we know is more likely to maintain motivation for many pupils, particularly those with low self-esteem and/or those who find school work difficult. It therefore addresses Wood's first criterion. It is possible to teach even young children (Tunstall and Gipps 1996a) as well as higher education students (Klenowski 1995, 1996) to monitor and manage their own learning in this way. The point is to plan-in opportunities for pupils to assess their own learning during the process of teaching and learning (Broadfoot 1996a). Training pupils' metacognitive strategies in this way, Broadfoot argues, empowers the pupil as an autonomous learner.

Reflection and discussion between pupil and teacher supports the learning process, motivation and metacognition. However, only if there is a real, rather than token, degree of responsibility for the student and real negotiation will learning to learn be fostered. And deliberate, reflexive self-evaluation must be embedded within a context that appreciates the difficulties in specifying 'quality' in learning, an ability that some argue is essentially intuitive (Claxton 1995).

TEACHER ASSESSMENT

Teacher assessment – which is also called *continuous assessment* or *school-based assessment* – refers to any informal or semi-formal assessment carried out by teachers within their classes. The purpose may be record-keeping, grading, or feedback to the pupil to aid learning or to the teacher to aid curriculum/lesson planning. Methods used may include questioning, observation, evaluation of written work, settings of tests and assessment tasks. The older the pupils, the more likely this assessment is to be based on written tasks and tests.

Teacher assessment is a key part of the teacher's repertoire: the teacher needs to know whether pupils are learning and making suitable progress. It also links with psychological research on '*match*': for effective learning, tasks must be pitched appropriately: at the current level to provide practice, or slightly higher to extend the pupil. If tasks are regularly too easy, the pupil will become bored; if too hard, the pupil may become demotivated.

Such assessment may also be called *formative assessment*, but we prefer to use this term in a rather narrowly defined way: teacher assessment is formative *only if the information feeds back into the teaching-learning process*. Some believe that assessment is only truly formative if it involves the pupil, others that it can be a process which involves only the teacher, who feeds the information back into curriculum and lesson planning.

In Sadler's classic paper (1989) formative assessment is connected with feedback, and for him feedback to teacher and pupil are separated:

> *Teachers use feedback to make programmatic decisions with respect to readiness, diagnosis and remediation. Students use it to monitor the strengths and weaknesses of their performances, so that aspects associated with success or high quality can be recognised and reinforced, and unsatisfactory aspects modified or improved.*
>
> (p.120)

Sadler's work started from the 'common but puzzling' observation that even when teachers give students valid and reliable judgments about their work, improvement does not necessarily follow. It seems that in order for the student to improve, he or she must have: a notion of the desired standard or goal, and be able to compare the actual performance with the desired performance and to engage in appropriate action to close the gap between the two. Feedback from the teacher, which helps the student with the second of these stages, needs to be of the kind and detail which tells the student what to do to improve: the use of grades or 7/10 marking cannot do this. Grades may in fact shift attention away from the criteria and be counter-productive for formative purposes.

This view of formative assessment is concerned with how judgments about the quality of students' responses can be used to shape and improve their competence by short-circuiting the randomness and inefficiency of trial-and-error learning. The key difference between formative assessment and summative assessment is not, therefore, timing, but purpose and effect: assessments made *during* the course of a unit or session may be used for summative or grading purposes rather than for truly formative purposes.

Formative assessment therefore fits in to constructivist approaches to learning with interaction between pupil and teacher supporting the child in learning (Torrance 1993).

There is sometimes confusion over the terms *formative assessment*, *summative assessment* and *teacher assessment* (indeed, the Dearing Review of the National Curriculum and Assessment used *formative assessment* and *teacher assessment* interchangeably). One way to get clarity into the definition is to emphasise that the terms relate not to the assessment themselves, but to the use made of the information (Wiliam and Black 1996). The same teacher assessment evidence may be used formatively or summatively; in order for the information to be used formatively it must be at an appropriate time and fed back in an appropriate way to allow the pupil to close the gap. We can therefore define *formative* assessment *in terms of its consequences or impact*. To be summative the assessment would be used to record the overall achievement of the pupil in a systematic way. Thus a level score from a key stage test is a summative assessment.

As Wiliam and Black remind us, however, '*whatever the labels that are used to describe it, formative assessment itself is, of course, nothing new.*

Almost all successful teaching . . . relies heavily on adapting the teaching in the light of evidence about the success of previous episodes' (1996, p.538).

Formative assessment: examples from primary practice

In a research project *Teacher Feedback to Young Children*[1] we looked at feedback from teachers to children in the process of formative assessment. Feedback from teachers to primary-aged pupils has three main functions: as part of the classroom socialisation process (*'I'm only helping people who are sitting down with their hands up'*); to encourage children and maintain motivation and effort, (*'beautiful work!', 'I think in fact this is probably the best one I've seen so far'*) and to identify specific aspects of attainment or good performance in relation to the task in hand. All the research on teaching and assessment, as well as common sense, tells us that this third function of feedback is vital for the teaching-learning process. Without it, children do not know how they are doing in relation to the task and, more importantly, what to do to improve – in other words, how they 'close the gap' between current performance and desired performance.

In the research we observed a wide range of feedback practice in Year 1 and Year 2 classes and the researchers discussed them with both teachers and children. On the basis of this work, a typology of assessment was developed (see Tunstall and Gipps 1996a,b for full details).

In Table 2.2, the first two columns can be seen to be concerned with maintaining motivation and encouraging effort; we term these *evaluative*. It is the types of feedback which focus on attainment, achievement and improvement that are particularly important in helping children to understand what is correct or good in their work and what needs to be done to improve. These we term *descriptive*.

Specifying attainment is teacher feedback which identifies specific aspects of successful attainment often following a *'mastery of small steps in learning approach'*, while *specifying improvement* identifies where mistakes lie and how work can be improved. In both these types the feedback is directed from the teacher to the child, with the teacher telling the child what is good or present in the work/activity and what can be done to improve.

The fourth column represents a collaboration between teacher and learner: *constructing achievement* is teacher feedback which is qualitatively different from *specifying attainment* – the description is undertaken much more in conversation or discussion with the child. Teachers using this type of feedback conveyed a sense of work in progress, heightening awareness of what was being undertaken and reflecting on it; it seemed to have the effect of bestowing importance on the child's work. Teachers' use of this feedback

[1]ESRC Ref: R00023 3780

Table 2.2 Typology of teacher feedback

	TYPE A	TYPE B	TYPE C	TYPE D	
	Rewarding	**Approving**	**Specifying attainment**	**Constructing achievement**	
1 **POSITIVE FEEDBACK**	rewards	positive personal expression	specific acknowledgement of attainment	mutual articulation of achievement	**1** **ACHIEVEMENT FEEDBACK**
		warm expression of feeling	use of criteria in relation to work/behaviour; teacher models	additional use of emerging criteria; child role in presentation	
		general praise	more specific praise	praise integral to description	
		positive non-verbal feedback			
	Punishing	**Disapproving**	**Specifying improvement**	**Constructing the way forward**	
2 **NEGATIVE FEEDBACK**	punishments	negative personal expression	correction of errors	mutual critical appraisal	**2** **IMPROVEMENT FEEDBACK**
		reprimands; negative generalisations	more practice given; training in self-checking	provision of strategies	
		negative non-verbal feedback			
	Evaluative		**Descriptive**		

LIVERPOOL JOHN MOORES UNIVERSITY
LEARNING SERVICES

shifted the emphasis to the child's own role in learning using approaches which seemed to pass some control to the child. It was less of 'teacher to the child' and more of 'teacher with the child'. With this type of feedback, teachers drew the child into explaining or demonstrating achievement using the child's own work; it also drew on and developed children's own self-assessment.

Constructing the way forward was used by teachers to articulate future possibilities in a learning partnership with the child, and it was carried out in a way that gave children greater responsibility. A key approach was to suggest that instead of telling children what to do to improve, the development was best identified mutually in such a way that children had more space to make choices for themselves. There was a feeling of teachers participating as learners in the classroom; the feedback was of a type where the teachers seemed to act as facilitators, making suggestions and questioning as part of discussion, rather than directing. This type of feedback provided children with strategies that they could adopt to develop their work, and it encouraged children to assess their own work.

The feedback typology is a useful tool for thinking about classroom practice: it gives us a language to use in discussing feedback and gives teachers a framework to use in reflecting on their feedback strategies. All these types of feedback are important in teaching and learning, but the balance is crucial. All learners, of whatever age, need the same things: clearly described goals and/or tasks; praise and reward; recognition of achievement; and clear information, or guidance, on what might be done to improve. Good formative assessment and feedback will feed in to good teaching and learning (see also Gipps 1997).

Learning through assessment

To come back to the argument at the beginning of this chapter about the relationship between assessment and learning, it seems that in order to encourage and support a mix of learning approaches we need to employ a mix of assessment approaches. For example, classroom tests are a quick and efficient way of testing recall of simple facts (e.g. number bonds, foreign language vocabulary), and basic skills (e.g. multiplication, spelling). Tests which require the pupil to write an answer, do practical tasks and projects (whether as part of a timed test or examination, coursework, or as part of everyday classroom assessment) are however better able to assess understanding and to encourage a deeper level of learning. Most importantly, if understanding is to be assessed, methods are required that involve the learners in applying their knowledge and linking it to real contexts. Understanding cannot be assessed by asking for the recall of isolated, decontextualised pieces of information; this will in any case shift teaching and learning away from understanding towards the memorisation of the information necessary to succeed in the assessment. Finally, for the teacher to know where the pupil is in his or her progress, informal observing, questioning and use of assessment tasks on a regular basis is important; this 'teacher assessment' has the key features of informality and regularity so assessments are made across contexts and time to build up a more complete picture than in a one-off test or examination.

Higher-order skills such as analysis, interpretation, critique, synthesis, applying knowledge and skills to new tasks, and constructing a convincing argument, are complex activities which cannot be assessed in simple ways that involve ticking answers which can be machine-scored. Part of our challenge for the new millennium is to teach such higher-order skills to a much broader range of students than in the past. Assessment of meaning and understanding is crucial in developing such skills.

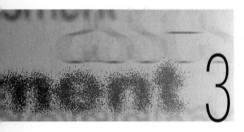

Monitoring and comparing performance

3

In the Introduction we identified the major uses of assessment and grouped them as contributing to either assessment **for** learning or to assessment **of** learning. We have emphasised the importance of teachers' formative assessment as something which is central to effective learning – and which is easily neglected when so much attention is given to the summative assessment of learning through national tests and examinations.

A new role for assessment has, however, emerged recently. Assessment is being used around the developed world to 'gear up' education systems in response to global changes. Economics drive the rhetoric: technological developments demand better educated, more thoughtful and flexible workers across the labour market, to strengthen the country's technological base and to foster a spirit of enterprise and initiative. The apparent mismatch between the output of the schools and the needs of the labour market in the 1980s, as indicated by the number of unqualified school leavers and by the number of young unemployed in various countries, suggested that education had departed from the 'real world' of work. The result has been to seek to recouple education with the economy (Neave 1988). A key component in this role for assessment is the use of national and international testing programmes to monitor performance – and competitiveness.

This chapter looks at what is currently the most public use of assessment: its use to *monitor* and *compare* educational performance. We have selected three high-profile forms of monitoring performance: the use of league tables and value-added measures to compare schools' performance; comparisons of standards over time; and monitoring national standards through international comparisons. The issue of comparable standards across qualifications, examination boards and syllabuses is tackled in chapter 7.

Comparing school performance

Currently one of the main uses of examination and national curriculum results is to monitor performance of schools and colleges. We use *school performance* as shorthand for any comparisons between institutions (for example, FE colleges, universities) or between local education authorities. While the data used may vary, the issues remain the same whether the comparison is between classes in the same school, between schools, or between local education authorities.

Reporting examination results

There has been a longstanding tradition of reporting 16+ and 18+ examination results in local newspapers, often naming the students. The 1980 Education Act formalised this by requiring all secondary schools to publish examination results from 1982 onwards. This Act was the first of the then-new Conservative government's moves in education, and a major plank was that parents using the state sector should have more information and choice in deciding which schools their children would attend.

Reaction to this requirement was mixed: several teachers' unions objected on professional grounds, believing that the published information was likely to be misleading and to have a negative effect on schools. Local authority organisations argued that the expense of providing the information could not be justified. On the other hand, there was a widespread belief that schools should be more accountable to the communities they serve and that the publication of examination results would help to bring this about.

The 1980 legislation did not, however, lay down the precise form in which the results had to be presented, which meant that schools soon engaged in forms of 'creative accounting' in order to present the results in the best light. The percentage of those passing, for example, may have been calculated for those who actually *sat* the examination rather than for those who were entered, some of whom may not have turned up.

The increased stress on public reporting of results led the government to look for 'fireproof' requirements which ensure that all schools report on the same basis. These were laid down in Circular 7/92 and involve detailed breakdown of statistics and performances, including the number of pupils by age group, the number in each year and the number absent from examinations. In addition, the national averages for that year's GCSE results, in each of the subjects taken, have to be reported, so that direct comparison can be made between school and national performance; this information must also be included in the school's prospectus.

Performance tables

In November 1992, national summary information in the form of percentages of pupils gaining five GCSE grades A–C and A–G was first published, by LEA and by school. This was a high-profile exercise (with some high-profile problems) with publishing costs of over £3 million. It was hailed by the then-Secretary of State as the fruit of the Parents' Charter. The tables have been produced annually since 1992 and are now a regular media event: 'now the tables are as much a part of the autumn term as harvest festivals and Christmas play rehearsals' (*Independent*, 14 November 1996).

While these tables contain more information than the percentage of students passing five GCSE grades A–C (see Table 3.1), their use by the media has quickly boiled down to ranking them on this basis, and the term *league tables* soon stuck as a name.

Examination league tables are now a fact of life and few politicians would dare to oppose them. There is, however, widespread concern about their misinterpretation and unfairness. An example of the latter is the direct comparison of the raw results of highly selective schools and of non-selective inner-city schools in the same authority. For instance, the 1996 league tables showed that within the Inner London borough of Southwark there were three schools with 97+% of their students gaining 5+ GCSEs at grades A*–C, with the other 14 secondary schools all scoring below 50%. It will come as no surprise to learn that the first three schools are prestigious private schools.

While common sense will lead us to make allowances for the type of school, there is a potentially more damaging misinterpretation which the presentation of league tables encourages. This is to *overrate the significance of the differences between schools' results*. At the heart of this misinterpretation is a lack of appreciation of the arbitrariness of the rank order. This does not mean the percentages are inaccurate, but rather that small differences within individual students' results can lead to large overall changes in the ranking of a school. This can be demonstrated by a hypothetical example. School Y has 100 examination students, of whom 40 gain five grades A*–C, putting the school below the national average (44.5%). The local press names it as a 'below average' school. Ten of the other students had four grades A*–C and at least one grade D. Had these ten students got three more marks in their grade D subject (i.e. enough to move them to a grade C), the school would have had a 50% success rate and been treated as 'above average'. It would also have moved up dozens, possibly hundreds, of places in any national rank order.

It is this kind of variability which leaves statisticians very cautious about making comparisons based on relatively small differences. When Harvey Goldstein and Desmond Nuttall (*Guardian*, 20 October 1992) used such data to make comparisons, they suggested that it was only the schools in the top and bottom 25% of the distribution that could be reliably compared. The overlap between the middle 50% of schools is so great that,

Table 3.1

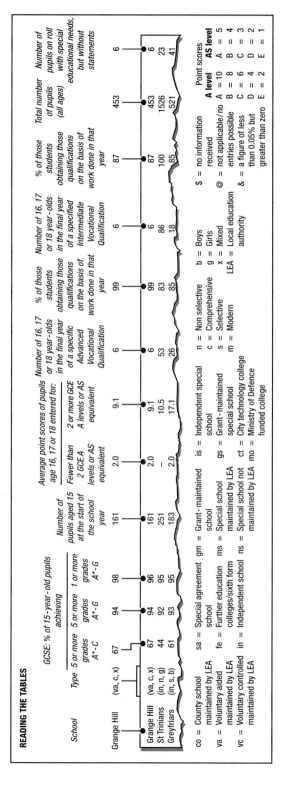

READING THE TABLES

School	Type	GCSE: % of 15-year-old pupils achieving			Number of pupils aged 15 at the start of the school year	Average point scores of pupils age 16, 17 or 18 entered for:		Number of 16, 17 or 18 year-olds in the final year of a specific Advanced Vocational Qualification	% of those students obtaining those qualifications on the basis of work done in that year	Number of 16, 17 or 18 year-olds in the final year of a specified Intermediate Vocational Qualification	% of those students obtaining those qualifications on the basis of work done in that year	Total number of pupils (all ages)	Number of pupils on roll with special educational needs, but without statements
		5 or more grades A*-C	5 or more grades A*-G	1 or more grades A*-G		Fewer than 2 GCE A levels or AS equivalent	2 or more GCE A levels or AS equivalent						
Grange Hill	(va, c, x)	67	94	98	161	2.0	9.1	6	99	6	87	453	6
Grange Hill	(va, c, x)	67	94	96	161	2.0	9.1	6	99	6	87	453	6
St Trinians	(in, n, g)	44	92	95	251	–	10.5	53	83	86	100	1526	23
Greyfriars	(in, s, b)	61	93	95	183	2.0	17.1	26	85	18	85	521	41

co = County school maintained by LEA
va = Voluntary aided maintained by LEA
vc = Voluntary controlled maintained by LEA

sa = Special agreement school
fe = Further education colleges/sixth form
in = Independent school

gm = Grant-maintained school
ms = Special school maintained by LEA
ns = Special school not maintained by LEA

is = Independent special school
gs = Grant-maintained special school
ct = City technology college
mo = Ministry of Defence funded college

n = Non selective
c = Comprehensive
s = Selective
m = Modern

b = Boys
g = Girls
x = Mixed
LEA = Local education authority

$ = no information received
@ = not applicable/no entries possible
& = a figure of less than 0.05% but greater than zero

Point scores

	A level	AS level
A	= 10	= 5
B	= 8	= 4
C	= 6	= 3
D	= 4	= 2
E	= 2	= 1

Source: The Guardian

as we have seen, small changes in a few results would reverse league positions. This also means that schools must expect year-by-year fluctuations in results over which they have little control, given that these may depend on the examination-day performance of a handful of students (*'you can take a horse to water'* . . .).

IMPROVING RESULTS

There is general agreement that league tables provide useful information and make schools more accountable. The question of whether they *improve* standards is more difficult. The logic is that schools want to be seen to get better results and therefore they will work harder for them. Thus the most improved (in league-table terms) secondary school in England in 1996 reported that: *'We sat down and analysed our results, where there were strengths and where there were weaknesses.'* The school then began to monitor every student and ensured that those giving cause for concern were kept on track. It introduced twice-weekly staff meetings and redirected resources. The proportion of pupils getting five or more higher-grade GCSEs leapt from 29% to 61% ('In the open', *Independent*, 14 November 1996).

While it is undoubtedly the case that schools will try to get better results because of the pressures of the league tables, some of the techniques may have less to do with overall improvement in teaching and learning than with playing the system. This may involve switching examination boards in order to find syllabuses that produce better results. It is more likely to involve targeting 'borderline' grade C students and giving them additional counselling, individual support and, on occasions, extra tuition ('Competition helps boost GCSE grades', *TES*, 29 November 1996). The research reported also found that these students were being entered for more subjects, and schools were trying to recruit more able pupils. While boosting borderline students may represent welcome attention for those who may previously have been neglected in the chase for the higher grades, there is concern that this is at the expense of lower-achieving students (8% of whom are leaving without *any* GCSEs) who are being entered for fewer subjects in the hope of a few better grades. Alan Smithers (1993) has proposed that, in order to encourage teachers to help weak candidates to catch up rather than to ignore them, league tables should be based on the *average* points score per pupil.

Similar pressures are at work with A level results. In 1996 the head of Cheltenham College, a prestigious independent school, was sacked because the school had slumped in the A level table. His crime had been to care as much about the achievements of his less able students as those who were strong examination candidates (of whom half got A or B grades and 20 went on to Oxbridge). His colleague Martin Stephen, High Master of Manchester Grammar School – a star performer in all tables – offered him the following tongue-in-cheek advice to improve league table position:

❝*There are four distinct types or categories of league table available to the consumer. All can be fiddled.*

[For DFEE tables] ... Lesson number one for the head who is keen to succeed is to enter everyone who can spell their own name for General Studies A level. It boosts the score beyond belief.

[For those tables based on the Independent Schools Information Service data] ... Persuade the top half of your pupils to go for four A levels. Since they work by adding up the total points score achieved and dividing it by the number of pupils sitting A levels, you do not need a GCSE in mathematics to work this one out.

Make every one of your pupils sit an AS level, regardless of whether they want to or not.

If you have been a good head, you have probably allowed any student to stay on in your sixth form who is working reasonably hard, even if an F grade will be a major achievement. This must change immediately: the pupil who will be lucky to get an F grade simply has to go. And while you are at it, refuse your weaker candidates the right to sit A levels with you.

('How to look good in league tables', *The Times*, 1 November 1996)

Lighthearted, of course, though Martin Stephen (whose school came top of the GCSE league tables in 1996) has also made a much more serious point:

League tables are a cancer on the body of education ... they have become an illness bringing irreparable harm by bringing in huge amounts of bad practice. They put pressure on schools to enter good pupils for an unnecessary number of exams. That's not education – that's cramming.

(*TES*, 27 December 1996, p.5)

NATIONAL CURRICULUM PERFORMANCE TABLES
The 1992 Schools Act gave the Secretary of State the powers to publish information which is likely to:

▶ **assist parents in choosing schools for their children;**

▶ **increase public awareness of the quality of education provided by the schools concerned and of the educational standards achieved in these schools (Section 16).**

In practice, there has been little consistency in what results have been reported. The original proposals were for reporting school results at 11, 14 and 16 years (Key Stages 2–4). LEA league tables for 7 year olds (Key

Stage 1) were published in 1991. Teacher action over the next few years (see chapter 6) meant results were withheld. Sir Ron Dearing, in his 1994 review of the national curriculum, recommended that league tables of schools should *not* be published for 7 and 14 year olds.

However, in February 1997 John Major made high-profile announcements that national performance tables would be published for 7, 11, 14 and 16 year olds. In March 1997 the first tables for 11 year olds were published, despite earlier caution from his ministers ('*We will introduce performance tables showing 11 year olds' test results for individual schools once the assessment arrangements have bedded in*' – Gillian Shephard, January 1996). The tables cover 18,500 schools and therefore over-simplification is inevitable: most show only the test results and not the teacher assessments. The value of *national* tables is far from obvious, given that parents are likely to be interested in *local* comparisons. To this end the Conservatives also announced that schools and local education authorities would have to set targets for improvement. The Labour Party indicated that they would publish them within LEAs.

We question the value, and expense, of such tables. Part of any discussion of the validity of a test is the *use* to which the results are put (see chapter 4). There is a particular concern at 11, since the evidence is that receiving secondary schools largely ignore the Key Stage 2 test results, so that the only use is likely to be in evaluating school performance, for which these count as a very blunt instrument. While there may be some value in seeing where a school is in relation to local performance and overall national performance, there seems little justification for a compendium of individual school results. This is particularly so if they are recast as league tables – since the measurement problems we raised in relation to examination league tables will be magnified at this level: many primary schools will be reporting on relatively small numbers of pupils at 7 and 11, with the result that the performance of a few borderline pupils will dramatically affect a school's average. This problem will be compounded by the insensitivity of the ten-level reporting scale. At 7 years virtually all pupils will be at levels 1–3, with the majority on level 2. With one level representing two years' progress, any effects of wrongly assigning levels are again magnified.

We also know that parents look at a variety of factors in choosing a primary school, including how close it is and whether they think their child would be happy there. Given all this, national league tables at 7, in particular, do not seem an efficient use of resources.

Value-added

If performance tables were seen as the way to accountability and improvement in the early 1990s then *value-added* is the current rallying call. What is meant by value-added is that results are presented in a way which takes account of what the school has contributed to the students'

progress. This is usually talked of in terms of *input* and *output* measures –
for example, students who enter the school at aged 11 at national
curriculum level 3 and who attain level 6 by 14 years may have done better
in value-added terms than students entering another school with level 5
and attaining level 7 at 14. In terms of raw results the second school would
be treated as performing better – even though it had done less for its
students. We would not want to give the impression that value-added is a
recent idea. The school effectiveness movement has been looking at this for
over thirty years, under the less catchy title of *'differential school
effectiveness'* (Gray 1996).

The move to value-added is therefore a logical response to the limitations
of the current reporting of raw test scores. Common sense tells us that we
should expect good results from academically selective schools and that
non-selective inner city schools are likely to be at the foot of the league
tables. What we want to know in judging a school is what has been added
to pupils' achievements since those pupils arrived. Looking at results in
this context could lead us to conclude that a school with unimpressive final
results has in fact done a very good job for the pupils who arrived with
limited skills and attainments at ages 5 or 11.

It is worth remembering that it was only in 1991 that the pioneering
value-added work of Nuttall and Goldstein was publicly ridiculed by the
then-Secretary of State, Kenneth Clarke. Before that, the TGAT report had
considered whether national curriculum results should be 'adjusted' to take
account of socio-economic and other factors. The report offered a 'lesser evil'
choice: the use of such results *'would be liable to lead to complacency if the
results were adjusted and to misinterpretation if they were not'* (TGAT 1988)
– and then opted for misinterpretation. It is now hard to find a
commentator for whom value-added is not 'a good thing'.

The basic issue for value-added is how to measure it. This means finding
'performance indicators' which reflect the quality of a school and yet which
can be straightforwardly reported. Those who have been working on
performance indicators and school effectiveness longest are amongst the
most cautious in putting forward any simple solutions:

> ❛*The search for a straightforward way of measuring the
> value-added by a school has every statistician in the
> business involved in the quest for this holy grail. . . . What we
> cannot expect is that it will be easy, or that any of the multi-
> levelled jargon pouring forth from competing researchers
> will convincingly untangle prior attainment from social
> factors from school effect.* ❜
>
> (*TES*, 25 November 1994)

If the lesson from league tables is the danger of over-simplification, we will
have to brace ourselves for some complexity. Desmond Nuttall was
unapologetic about this:

> **'***Don't be frightened by a bit of complexity. We've learnt to live with seasonally adjusted unemployment figures, a Retail Price Index that includes both rent and mortgages . . . an incredibly complicated Rate Support Grant Settlements. . . . I believe we can learn to live with appropriate complexity in 'value-added'.***'**
>
> (Nuttall 1993, p.31)

At its most basic, value-added measures the progress shown using measures of attainment on entry and on leaving. The school can then be given appropriate credit for extending pupils' attainment. A relatively simple form of this is to take pupils' GCSE grades in conjunction with their A level grades to determine how much 'value' the A level courses added. Thus a school with unspectacular A level results from pupils with limited success at GCSE may be found to have achieved more than a 'high flying' school which achieved good A level results from pupils who had excellent GCSE results.

Government plans to use pupils' national curriculum levels at ages 7 and 11 as a baseline for 'value-added' were proposed in 1993 (it will be 1999 before secondary schools can be similarly assessed). It is unlikely that such analyses will be sophisticated: *'The Secretary of State will want any such measures to be few, straightforward and intelligible to parents'* (DFE, 21 October 1992).

However, there are problems in using school results achieved after adjustment, as they can vary considerably and apparently haphazardly by making trivial modifications to the adjustment procedures. Goldstein and Woodhouse (1988) found this for LEAs; the same effect has been found in ranking school districts (rather than schools) in Kentucky: changing or modifying criteria for ranking and for adjusting scores resulted in quite different rankings of school districts (Guskey and Kifer 1989). It is also the case that rank order can change quite considerably from one year to the next. Furthermore, the limitation with ranking as a process is that, regardless of overall levels of performance, a ranking procedure always produces a top and a bottom, with little indication of what these mean in terms of performance. As the Kentucky study puts it: *'The ten shortest players in the National Basketball Association, for instance, are on average pretty tall.'*

Using a new statistical method, each child's performance can be analysed in relation to his or her gender, ethnic group, attainment on entry to school, etc, rather than, as before, school average performance being analysed against school measures of its population. Multi-level modelling techniques (Goldstein 1987) allow the information about individual pupil attainment and characteristics to be analysed together with school level data, thus giving a much more sophisticated picture of how well schools are producing good results for certain groups of pupils. Some inner-London schools were found to be more effective than others at improving the performance of lower-ability pupils, and of some groups of ethnic minority students (Nuttall *et al* 1989).

More recent and more widely-based work, however, suggests that as a general rule schools that are effective are effective for all groups of pupils. It is unusual to find a school that improves the performance of girls but not boys, or the more able but not the less able. (See Mortimore *et al* 1994 and Gray 1996, who provide very readable reviews.)

It is clear that there is currently considerable political and educational support for value-added approaches. There will inevitably be pressure for 'simple' measures – which will present us with the same league-table problems that they were meant to solve. Perhaps we should insist on some complexity and resist any attempt at ranking schools: *'the majority of schools achieve precisely the sort of results one would predict from their intakes . . . "effectiveness" is not a precisely estimable quantity'* (Gray 1996).

We return to value-added in the final chapter. We emphasise that it is not sufficient for a school to 'add value', however impressively, if the pupils who leave have still not achieved the appropriate skills to progress to the next phase of education or into the workforce.

Comparing standards over time

There is an abiding concern that standards are not what they used to be. Alan Bennett captures this nicely:

> ❝**Parent**: *Have you thought, Headmaster, that your standards might be a little out of date?*
> **Headmaster**: *Of course they are out of date. Standards always are out of date. That's what makes them standards.* ❞
> (Alan Bennett, *Forty Years On*)

The dilemma in measuring changes over time is to find a methodology which can take account of the changes to the student population, the curriculum, teaching styles, and assessment techniques so that a judgement can be made. For many researchers this is seen as so problematic that they feel it is not worth attempting:

> ❝*The measurement of change in the level of performance of educational systems is not possible as there is no way of establishing an unchanging measuring instrument over any length of time. Indeed, there are dangers in attempting so to do, because such a measuring instrument cannot adapt to meet current needs or concerns.* ❞
> (Nuttall 1995, p.129)

In practice such studies get done because of a political imperative which overrides problems with method. A recent example of this was *Standards in Public Examinations 1975 to 1995*, a report jointly produced by OFSTED and SCAA in December 1996. The study was a response to ministerial concern that the increased pass rates in the 1995 GCE A level and GCSE examinations may have represented a dilution of examination standards rather than improvements in students' performance.

The study covered three subjects at both levels: English, mathematics and science. It considered two aspects of examination standards:

▶ **examination standards refer to the demands of syllabuses and their assessment arrangements, and the levels of performance required of candidates to gain particular grades;**

▶ **standards of attainment refer to the knowledge, understanding and skills that candidates demonstrate in examinations (p.1).**

The task was therefore to judge whether the examination was more or less demanding than in earlier years, and whether the same level of performance at a given grade boundary was equivalent to that required in earlier years. In order to judge the latter a review of examination scripts had to be carried out.

The description of the 'evidence base' underlines the problems: speaking and listening was introduced as a new component in the GCSE English; no examination boards could provide scripts from the 1970s and few from the 1980s; no coursework was available before 1990; there was insufficient evidence to make any comparisons of O level and GCSE, so instead the 1990 and 1995 GCSEs were compared, though without reference to coursework. There was also a problem caused by changes in entry patterns. For example, the proportion of 18–19 year olds going into higher education was 14% in 1975 and 31% in 1995. During this period there was also a dramatic increase in the number of females taking A levels. These examples illustrate the difficulty, if not impossibility, of comparing 'like with like'.

The conclusions drawn from both strands of the study were understandably tentative. There was clearly evidence of change in each subject, so much so in English at 16+ that the conclusion was *'that such changes make it difficult to reach firm conclusions about standards over time'* (p.19). The most common refrain from each subject and level was that, while there had been changes in content, the level of demand on candidates remained broadly similar. There were subject-specific concerns such as the reduction of algebraic content in mathematics (offset by increased data handling) and the lack of fluency in describing chemical reactions and concepts – which the chemistry specialists did not want to be offset by the increased emphasis on application of knowledge.

The tentativeness of the findings was not reflected in the scale and nature of the action which has followed. Even though there was *'no hard evidence that standards are falling'*, the then-Secretary of State Gillian

Shephard announced a package of measures to *'ensure standards remain steady'*. The reasoning for this was that *'there has been a change in the nature of examinations'* and some of the changes in course content were unacceptable (*op cit*). These measures included:

▶ **increased emphasis on spelling, punctuation and grammar in A level and GCSE English and a new GCSE in English language from September 1998;**

▶ **more pre-1900 literature in A level English;**

▶ **reduced use of calculators in mathematics at A level and GCSE, including calculator-free papers;**

▶ **fewer examination boards and syllabuses;**

▶ **a national archive of papers and scripts.**

The issue of limiting change in curriculum and therefore examinations in order to 'maintain' standards takes us back to Nuttall's objections to this type of study. The 'dangers' of the measuring instrument not adapting to current needs may be illustrated by the move back to calculator-free mathematics papers or increased emphasis on pre-nineteenth-century literature in examinations designed to take us into the next century.

Colin Goldsmith, who was responsible for the mathematics section of the report, sees these proposals as a misinterpretation of the main message in his part of the report ('Old gold standard fails to pay', *TES*, 14 February 1997). He reminds us that in 1975, in the syllabuses reviewed, 44% of A level mathematics candidates failed. This was because the examination did not change at a time when university expansion saw many more students taking mathematics. This mismatch between candidates and examination received negligible publicity:

❛*The moral to this story is obvious: that any institution must adapt to altering circumstances. School assessment is no exception. When the clientele for A level mathematics changed, the examinations had to change too. Courses should always be challenging, but tailored to the needs and abilities of the students for whom they are intended. This fosters motivation and leads to more effective teaching and learning. It maximises real attainment. Over-hard assessment merely discourages and shows up candidates' deficiencies; ideal assessment reveals accurately what students know and can do. No politician in any party has been brave enough to explain to the public that 'lower standards' are often appropriate and highly desirable, leading to what are, in some important respects, higher standards. Just as economists do not now argue for a rigid and immutable currency exchange rates, so educationalists should not entertain the chimera of an A level Gold Standard.*

> ... *Mathematics assessment at A level has become more accessible to weaker students (that is, easier); the motivation of students has increased; the passmark has risen; and failure rates have been further reduced. These factors are inter-related and it is unhelpful and irrelevant to try to sum them up in a crude statement such as 'standards have fallen'.* **"**
>
> *(op cit)*

The enigmatic reference to '*lower standards [leading to] in some important respects, higher standards*' needs some demystifying. We take this to mean, amongst other things, that part of raising standards is increasing the number of students who achieve them. If an examination is made easier but attracts many more students who are then successful, have not overall standards of performance been increased? One way of looking at this would be to say that we should be comparing the performance of students at 18 who were not in the top 25% of achievers in mathematics at 16 (i.e. grade C) with their equivalents of 20 years ago, very few of whom would have even taken an A level course. This, rather than comparing, at grade A, the top 10% of a highly selected and homogenous group with the top 20% of a larger and more diverse one, might help us grasp more easily how we can lower standards in order to raise them.

An analogy might also help. In 1953 Mount Everest was climbed for the first time by two climbers. On one single day in 1993, thirty-nine climbers reached the summit. What has happened to Mount Everest during this period? Develop the argument a little more and we find an assumption that climbing it has got 'easier' because of better routes, equipment and preparation. Scratch below the surface and we find a preference for the heroic amateur (cf. *Chariots of Fire*), overcoming inadequate equipment and support, to the well-prepared professional. Somehow '*climbing is not what it used to be*'.

Despite all these reservations, 'standards over time' studies will continue. While a national archive would produce more reliable evidence with which to work, this will not reduce the fundamental problem of taking account of change – within society, the curriculum and the students who take the course – in order to make fair comparisons.

International comparisons

There is a strong case that standards in relation to other competitor nations is a far more pressing issue than whether standards are better or worse than 20 years ago. This is increasingly important as '*Nations are more aware than ever before that their fortunes in the world depend on the educational levels of their populations. Average national school achievement is no longer merely a status symbol but, though crude, stands as one outstanding indicator of a nation's economic and social health*' (Eckstein 1996, pp.238–9). This belief fuels interest in international comparisons, and unwelcome findings from these will trigger national debate, usually of the 'where have we gone wrong' variety. A good example of this was the report of the US National Commission on Excellence in Education 1983, which used international comparisons to underline the poor performance of American students. It concluded:

> *❛If an unfriendly foreign power had attempted to impose on America the mediocre educational performance that exists today, we might well have viewed it as an act of war. As it stands, we have allowed this to happen to ourselves. . . .We have, in effect, been committing an act of unthinking, unilateral educational disarmament.❜*
>
> (p.5, quoted in Kellaghan 1996)

The response to such unfavourable comparisons has been for the US Department of Education to declare that '*By the year 2000, US students will be first in the world in science and mathematics achievement*' (1991). Perhaps teachers in the UK can take some comfort that this pattern of blame and promise happens elsewhere too.

Like other forms of comparison, the problem is once again how we measure it. Kellaghan (1996) has listed nine conditions that need to be met for international comparisons. Two of these are essential:

▶ **the data must accurately reflect what students achieve in individual countries;**

▶ **the tests fairly reflect the curricula of the countries involved, and the samples of pupils on which it is based are equivalent.**

This is clearly a tall order and all international comparisons will have problems fully meeting them. If curricula differ significantly, then it will be hard to produce valid tests. If the students are carefully selected in one country and conscripted in another, this undermines equivalence. (In the 1990 mathematics study, it was reported that Korean students marched to the test through streets lined with cheering classmates, whilst many American students volunteered only in order to get out of PE!) However, there is a growing sense that methodology is improving with each round of studies; the International Association for the Study of Educational Achievement (IEA) has now conducted twelve major studies since 1960 (see *Assessment in Education*, Volume 3, No. 2, 1996, for a full review of IEA work).

We consider that these studies are now sufficiently valid and reliable to take the findings seriously, though with the same health warnings as league tables when attempts are made to rank-order countries. In the 1996 study, the top four countries in mathematics were all Pacific Rim countries (Singapore, Korea, Japan and Hong Kong), the first three also featuring in science. In science, English pupils were ranked 11th, with Irish and Scottish pupils ranked 18th and 26th respectively. In mathematics, the positions were 23rd, 15th and 27th, respectively.

The key issue here is how to translate any findings into improved curricula and teaching. Even with the earlier and more unreliable studies, policy-makers used the results to make changes. Whether these changes to the curriculum were the most effective response has sometimes been debatable. In the First International Mathematics Study the United States' poor result is credited with the demise of the 'new math', whilst in Hungary, where students performed well on the mathematics tests, this was attributed to having discarded the teaching of traditional arithmetic and geometry in favour of 'new math'! (Kellaghan 1996).

Another relevant report is the OFSTED-commissioned comparison with the performance of pupils in Asia and other parts of Europe (Reynolds and Farrell 1996). This work has shown how the performance gap is widening between 9 and 13 year old English children and their peers in Pacific Rim countries such as Taiwan.

The key classroom differences are identified as:

> ▶ **the high proportion of lesson time spent on 'whole class interactive instruction', in which the teacher ensures all children have grasped the information given, instead of expecting them to work on their own;**
>
> ▶ **children all using the same textbooks;**
>
> ▶ **measures to ensure that the range of achievement is kept small, such as requiring pupils who have fallen behind to finish after school and even keeping them down a year;**
>
> ▶ **frequent testing of pupils' skills in core subjects;**
>
> ▶ **use of specialist teachers in primary schools;**
>
> ▶ **delaying the introduction of calculators.**

The problem with this type of comparison is that it easily degenerates into a 'shopping list' that is imported without fully considering the cultural context. This is not to say that we have nothing to learn from other countries, but that, before we introduce such changes, we should begin by questioning some of our basic assumptions which other cultures challenge.

The most fundamental assumption which such studies challenge is our deeply ingrained belief in the differences in *innate ability*. This Anglo-Saxon preoccupation, reflected in the history of intelligence testing, means that we accept wide differences in attainment and this can lead to low expectations of those who 'just haven't got it'. The current unpopularity of 'mixed-ability' teaching and preference for streaming seems to be predicated on just this.

In contrast, the Pacific Rim countries begin from a very different assumption: *'In the Confucian tradition the presumption is that everyone is educable. Although Confucius did not refuse to teach anybody on the basis of ability, he would, however, have refused to teach a person who was not eager to learn'* (Gipps, 'The paradox of the Pacific Rim learner', *TES*, 20 December 1996). This belief directly informs classroom practice: achievement is the product of effort rather than innate ability and all can succeed if they try. Whole-class 'mixed-ability' teaching follows on naturally from this (streaming is against the law in Taiwan). The social context in which this takes place is a culture which sees will-power as the driving force of effort, an attribute which is independent of background. The Confucian culture, too, means that pupils arrive at school socialised to become geared to diligent effort. This contrasts with efforts teachers may have to make in British, American or Australian classrooms in order to motivate children.

We have briefly looked at these two assumptions in order to emphasise the importance of not adopting techniques from elsewhere without deeper reflection of the context in which they are successful. David Reynolds, co-author of the OFSTED report, had to counteract simplistic interpretations of the classroom methods he advocated. Because traditionalists had not recognised the highly interactive style of the whole-class teaching, they assumed this was an invitation to return to teachers talking at classes of passive children and to rote learning drills:

> *'There is no evidence to support what the traditionalists are saying about the effectiveness of whole-class instruction. It is whole-class interactive instruction that is the key. Going reactively towards whole-class instruction is as silly as going to group work as a reaction against whole-class teaching.'*
> ('Going back to the future is wrong', *Independent*, 6 June 1996)

Our parting shot on the findings of such international comparisons concerns the status of the teacher – which is invariably higher in the countries we are seeking to emulate. John Townshend observes:

> *'Overall, what emerges is a picture of some convergence between those systems which formerly constrained teachers within a straitjacket of regulations and tightly controlled procedures but which are now relaxing these restraints and giving teachers more autonomy, and those previously decentralised systems, especially in the English-speaking world, which are now tightening their curricular and assessment procedures.... The paradox is that too much prescription of content and performance standards, especially when linked with high-profile reporting of test results, may damage teacher professionalism. Yet it is the high professional status and public esteem of teachers which seems to characterise those countries where student performance standards are highest.'*
> (Townshend 1996, p.11)

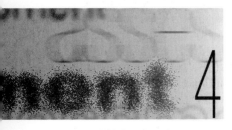

4 Measurement issues

In this book we have not taken the conventional approach of beginning with technical issues and definitions. We have looked rather at the broad assessment issues that teachers have to face in their work and that are raised in public and political debate. In this chapter we introduce some of the more technical issues around assessment. We begin by looking at two of the key assessment terms we have used loosely so far: *validity* and *reliability*. We then move on to measurement issues that have to be faced in any discussion of standards. The first of these is whether *norm-referenced* or *criterion-referenced* measures are being used, and the limitations of each. Linked to this is the issue of *over-simplifying* the presentation of results in order to provide easily understood information for parents. We then consider the effects of *high-stakes* assessment and possible alternatives.

Validity and reliability

In any discussion of the merits of a test or assessment regime, *validity* and *reliability* are frequently, and often loosely, used terms. While we describe some of the conventional formulations of these concepts, we also look at more recent definitions which take a much broader and more integrated approach.

Validity

The traditional definition of validity is the extent to which a test measures what it was designed to measure; if it does not measure what it purports to measure, then its use is misleading.

Early writings about validity emphasised four *types* of validity: predictive, concurrent, construct and content. **Predictive validity** relates to whether the test predicts accurately or well some future performance – for example, is A level a good predictor of performance in higher education?

One difficulty in calculating predictive validity is that, in this example, only those who pass the examination go on to university (generally speaking) and we do not know how well students who did *not* pass might have done (see Wood 1991). Also, only a small proportion of the population takes A level and the correlation between A level grades and degree performance would be higher if the entire 18-year-old population were included in the A level group.

Concurrent validity is concerned about whether the test correlates with, or gives substantially the same results as, another test of the same skill. Of course, if the second test is not itself valid (in terms of content or construct), then we may have simply two tests which correlate with each other but are not valid for the purpose intended. An example here would be a reading test which correlated highly with the *Schonell Graded Word Reading Test*, which we now see as having very low construct validity.

Construct validity itself relates to whether the test is an adequate measure of the construct – that is, the underlying (explanatory) skill being assessed. Important to the development of an assessment is a clear and detailed definition of the construct. For example, a full definition of reading as a construct would include not only reading aloud, but also reading comprehension, accuracy, and enjoyment of reading.

Content validity is more straightforward, and likely to stem from construct validity. It concerns the coverage of appropriate and necessary content – that is, does the test cover the skills necessary for good performance, or all the aspects of the subject taught? Content validity tends to be based on professional judgements about the relevance of the test content to the content of a particular domain – for example, measurement in mathematics – and the representativeness with which the content samples that domain.

Concurrent and predictive validity are often combined to give **criterion validity**, because they both relate to predicting performance on some criterion, either at the same time or in the future. There are other definitions of validity too (Wood 1987; Wiliam 1992), but those outlined above have been the main approaches.

Emphasis on these different types of validity has led to a situation in which, all too often, in test development evidence is provided about only one or two of these types of validity. More recently therefore the literature on validity has emphasised that validity is in fact a *unitary* concept (Messick 1989; Cronbach 1988). The responsibility for valid test use is put on to the *user*, not the test developer (assuming that there is evidence of construct validity).

VALIDITY AS A UNITARY CONCEPT

Messick (1989), in his classic chapter on validity, describes the testing profession's move to an approach in which:

> ❝for a fully unified view of validity, it must also be recognised that the appropriateness, meaningfulness and

usefulness of score-based inferences depend as well on the social consequences of the testing. Therefore, social values cannot be ignored in considerations of validity. **9**

(p.19)

Messick therefore is operating with a notion of validity that relates to inferences drawn from test scores:

6*Validity is an integrated evaluative judgement of the degree to which empirical evidence and theoretical rationales support the adequacy and appropriateness of influences and attitudes based on test scores or other modes of assessment.* **9**

(p.13)

Validity here, then, relates to the *evidence* available to support test interpretation and potential *consequences* of test use. This, clearly, is a different and more demanding conception of validity than '*the extent to which a test measures what it purports to measure*'. In practice, it means that even a well-constructed test is not valid if the results are used inappropriately: to use a maths test to select students for a Fine Art course, or a music test to select engineers, even if the tests are technically superb, provide extreme examples of how it is the *use* of test results which determines validity. The importance of this for teachers is that, in using test results, validity is an issue of professional responsibility rather than merely the concern of test developers.

Reliability

The traditional definitions of reliability focus on the *consistency* of results. A common definition would be that a test is reliable if two identical students got the same results. Since we do not have such students, we use other measures as a proxy for this: **test-retest reliability**, which is based on gaining the same marks if the test is repeated; **mark-remark reliability** which looks at the agreement between markers; and, **parallel forms/split-half reliability** in which similar tests give similar marks. Curiously, another form of reliability – **repeated measures** – is often neglected. This is unfortunate because, in discussing the reliability of coursework and of teacher assessment, the fact that performance is assessed on a number of occasions makes the measurement in this respect more reliable than a 'one-off' test. Indeed, the perception of examinations as reliable and coursework as unreliable usually has more to do with opinion than with evidence. It is often the case that the reliability of examinations is over-rated and that of coursework under-rated (see Satterly 1994, Wilmut *et al* 1996).

Whilst the first three forms of reliability are of importance to test developers, they are of little use to a classroom teacher. This is primarily because they work with average scores drawn from large groups. Thus a 'reliable' test may not in practice be a particularly reliable measure of an individual student. Dylan Wiliam, who provides a very readable introduction to these issues (Wiliam 1992), clarifies this by treating reliability as only a small part of the **dependability** of a test in providing accurate information about the performance of individual students. We deal with Wiliam's ideas in some detail, because they provide a more constructive and active approach than the customary treatment of reliability. For the teacher, he argues, it is more fruitful to work with the concepts of *disclosure* and *fidelity*:

❛*The* **disclosure** *of an assessment is the extent to which it produces evidence of attainment from an individual in the area being assessed. One way of asking a question might produce no answer from the student, from which a teacher might assume that the student did not have the attainment in question. However, when asked the question in a slightly different way, the student might well answer correctly. This effect is often particularly marked when we compare the responses to written test items with the results of a one-to-one conversation with a student. It is also possible that students actively suppress evidence of attainment, either because they think that what they have done is not appropriate, or, in some cases, because they do not want to appear too 'brainy'.*

In general, we should be very reluctant to conclude that our failure to elicit evidence of an attainment means that the student does not have that attainment: very often, all it means is that we haven't asked the question in the right way for that individual, and the verdict should be not proven. ❜

(*op cit*, p.13)

The **fidelity** of an assessment is the extent to which evidence of attainment that has been *disclosed* is recorded faithfully. There are three main ways this can go wrong: the evidence is not observed (e.g. the teacher was listening to another group at the time); the observation is incorrectly interpreted (e.g. it treats the achievement as at a lower level than is actually the case); and, it is observed and interpreted correctly but is not recorded – because the teacher is too busy.

In moving to a definition of validity which includes the use to which results are put, and in re-casting reliability as part of the dependability of assessments rather than a feature of test construction, we have sought to give both terms more relevance to the teacher's professional practice and to stimulate more constructive discussions of, in particular, what is meant by *valid* and *reliable* teacher assessment.

Norm-referenced measures

Most of the measures on which judgements about standards are made are norm-referenced. There is a real paradox here, because the key feature of norm-referenced assessment is that the grades, or the pass–fail cut-off, are assigned on the basis of a fixed proportion of candidates gaining them, rather than on a set number of marks. The value of norm-referenced measures lies in ranking students for selection; what such measures cannot do is give a clear indication of a student's actual attainments. For example, the grade A in a particular examination may only be awarded to the top 10% of the entry, irrespective of how good (or bad) the entry was. Thus the grade a student receives will depend directly on the quality of the *other* students, rather than simply on the quality of this student's work. The same work could get an A one year and a B the next, simply because of changes in the performance of the other candidates. Similarly, in American schools and colleges *'grading on the curve'* refers to the relatively fixed proportions of grades being distributed. The curve in question is a statistical one, the normal distribution curve, which assumes a regular 'bell-shaped' distribution of scores with the majority grouped around the mean and the distribution tailing off towards the extremes.

Standardised reading tests are an example of a norm-referenced test. In the development, or *standardisation*, of a test, a large sample of children of particular ages is used as a reference point. Subsequently, when a test is given to a child, his or her score (called *raw score*) is compared with this table of scores to give a *'standardised'* score, which indicates where the child stands in relation to the scores of the original large sample and therefore whether the child is average, above average or below average compared with this reference group. Usually 100 is given as the average, with a *standard deviation* of 15 – which means any standardised score between 85 and 115 (i.e. 100 plus or minus 15) is within the average range. About two-thirds of the full sample of children would fall into this range. Thus if a child has a raw score of 35 on a test, and this converts to a standardised score of 120, it would indicate above-average reading ability compared to other children of the same age. Scores on intelligence or reasoning tests are also usually calibrated in this way.

A **reading age** is a particular form of standardisation conversion. If, in the standardisation of the test, the average score for children aged 8 years and 6 months was 35, then any child who gets a raw score of 35 on that test would be said to have a reading age of 8 years and 6 months, regardless of his or her actual age.

GCE examinations are essentially norm-referenced. When the A level 'letter grades' were introduced, in 1963, there was an understanding that there would be stable proportions of candidates at each grade: 10% at A; 15% at B; 10% at C; 15% at D and 20% at E – giving a pass rate of 70%, the same as the High School Certificate it had replaced in 1951. Though this was couched in terms of '*all the above percentages are to be regarded as no more than rough indications*' (Secondary School Examinations Council 1960), stress was laid on the importance of ensuring that the proportion of candidates awarded a grade C was not allowed to deviate markedly from the suggested norm (Christie and Forrest 1981). GCSE examinations are also essentially norm-referenced, despite attempts to make them more criterion-referenced (see below). Indeed, GCE A level and GCSE are becoming more obviously norm-referenced, in that the proportions of candidates gaining particular grades are not allowed to fluctuate from year to year by more than a small percentage – typically 2% – without referring it to senior examination board personnel.

The dilemma here is how to judge whether standards have improved if the proportion of grades awarded stays the same, irrespective of changes in year-on-year performance by the candidates. In practice what happens is that these grade proportions do vary slightly from year to year, as examiners include considerations of the quality of the work in setting the marks for the grade boundaries. The problem, particularly when pass rates increase, is to decide whether this reflects a genuine improvement in the standard of the candidates' work or an easing of standards by the examination boards, for whom a low pass rate may affect future entries. Every August, as the GCE and then GCSE results are published, politicians and leader writers are left with the choice of whether to denounce or applaud an increased pass rate.

The 1992 GCSE results provide a classic case study of this problem. The overall GCSE results showed a 2.3% increase in grades A–C, to 51.3% (breaching the 50% barrier), and these were welcomed by junior minister Eric Forth (*Guardian*, 27 August 1992). However, in early September the government published an HMI report which cast doubt on the awarding procedures and reported only '*limited confidence*' in the results. The Secretary of State immediately ordered a review into this '*erosion of standards*' and the press revelled in the paradox of better results meaning falling standards. The GCSE examining groups then pointed out that HMI attendance at forty or so awarding meetings in 1992 gave them no real basis to compare standards with the previous years' awarding – at which they had not been present and for which procedures had been less standardised (*TES*, 11 September 1992). It is also worth noting that the 'non-privatised' HMI of Wales, Scotland and Northern Ireland all concluded that similar result patterns in these countries represented an *improvement* in standards.

National curriculum key stage tests are now conducted in a similar way to public examinations. The levels awarded in the tests are based on the students' total marks, with experts using 'expectations' of the distribution of levels to determine cut-off points for Levels on the mark scale. We are now also beginning to see arguments over whether changes in proportions of pupils at particular levels is the result of standards rising or the tests being leniently marked. As we shall see in the next section, this more norm-referenced approach was not the original intention for national curriculum assessment.

Criterion-referenced assessment

Criterion-referenced assessment was introduced as an educational alternative to norm-referenced psychometric measurement. It emergence is credited to Glaser, who defined it in terms of its difference from norm-referenced testing:

> ❛What I shall call criterion-referenced measures depend upon an absolute standard of quality, while what I term norm-referenced measures depend upon a relative standard. . . . Measures which assess student achievement in terms of a criterion standard thus provide information as to the degree of competence attained by a particular student which is independent of reference to the performance of others. ❜
>
> (Glaser 1963, pp.520–1)

What this boils down to in practice is that criterion-referenced approaches specify what needs to be done in order to qualify, and the student who meets these requirements will pass – independent of whether others do: 'Candidates' results should not be affected by the company they keep' (Wood 1991, p.122). A simple example is a swimming certificate. If a child swims the 20 metres then the certificate is hers, regardless of who else gets it. The norm-referenced equivalent would be a swimming trials from which the first three finishers qualify and the rest get nothing. It is important to recognise, however, that there are norm-referenced assumptions behind criterion-referenced measures. It would be foolish, for example, to set the criteria for the first music grade at a level which only accomplished musicians could attain, or for a driving test so that virtually nobody passed. The skill is to set criteria which are attainable by those for whom they are intended.

Criterion-referenced assessment has appealed to both educators and policy-makers. It should allow teachers to monitor and encourage individual achievement and direct tests at what has been learned. For policy-makers it means that clear information is available about what students can actually do. It should also allow judgements to be made about standards in a way that norm-referenced tests cannot.

In England there have been two interesting examples of attempts to introduce criterion-referenced assessment into the mainstream curriculum. The interest lies partly in the lack of success of the approach when it was applied to GCSE and to national curriculum assessment. We describe both attempts, as they point up some of the limitations of criterion-referencing. The more enduring use of criterion-referenced assessment in vocational qualifications is discussed in chapter 8.

GCSE and grade-related criteria

Specifying the criteria in criterion-referenced assessment is not always easy, and has proved to be a particular problem in GCSE. Sir Keith Joseph's announcement of the new GCSE in 1984 included a reference to *grade-related criteria* – the criteria which students would have to meet in order to gain a particular grade:

> *examination grades should have a clearer meaning, and pupils and teachers need clearer goals. We accordingly need grade-related criteria which will specify the knowledge, understanding and skills expected for the award of particular grades.*

> (DES 1987b)

One of the reasons for the interest of the DES and Secondary Examinations Council (SEC) in the development of criterion-referencing within GCSE was concern over comparability – or rather the lack of it – in GCSE grades from different boards. With a single, consistent, system of clearly defined grades, all the examination boards would apply the same standards in awarding grades (Orr and Nuttall 1983).

There were already *grade descriptions* in the GCSE subject criteria which gave a broad idea of the performance likely to have been shown by a candidate awarded a particular grade, but what was wanted were more specific descriptions of performance. So SEC set up working parties in each of the main subjects to develop *grade criteria*. These working parties first identified 'domains' – coherent and defined areas of knowledge, understanding and skills within each subject. The groups then broke the domains down into abilities and produced definitions of performance, or criteria, required for achievement at different levels.

The reaction to the draft grade criteria was largely negative. The main criticism was that they were far too complex (the mathematics group produced eighty detailed criteria for one domain at a single grade level). There was also a concern that breaking subjects down in this way would be counterproductive:

> *The rigorous specification of full criterion-referencing for assessment in the GCSE would result in very tightly defined syllabuses and patterns of assessment which would not allow the flexibility of approach that characterises education in this country.*

> (SEC 1984, p.2)

Thus the move to grade-related criteria was abandoned at an early stage. The exercise exemplified the tendency to over-complicate, through over-detailed criteria and assessment, the requirements of criterion-referenced assessment.

Criterion-referencing in the national curriculum

Those who have been teaching the national curriculum since it was introduced will be painfully aware of the repeated changes, not only to the content but also to the assessment criteria.

The framework for subject development and assessment was provided by the Task Group on Assessment and Testing (TGAT), which reported in 1988. The basic model was essentially a criterion-referenced one, which drew heavily on current 'graded assessment' schemes being developed by the Inner London Education Authority. The assumption was that subjects would be broken into domains and within each would be a sequence of carefully defined levels through which pupils would progress, moving on after they had mastered their current level. For the national curriculum this resulted in subjects being divided in *Profile Components* ('*preferably no more than four and never more than six*') which were then specified in terms of a *ten-level scale*. The normative element in this was that the levels were treated as age-related: the average child at 7 years would be at level 2, at 11 years level 4 and so on – progressing one level every two years. The top four levels would match the GCSE grades.

The assessments intended for this structure would be centrally devised standard assessment tasks (SATs) which would be used and marked by the class teacher. These were to:

> ❝*exploit a wide range (far wider than those normally envisaged for tests) of modes of presentation, operation and response, and their numerous combinations, in order to widen the range of pupils' abilities that they reflect and so to enhance educational validity.* ❞
>
> (TGAT Report, para. 48)

The aim here was to provide SATs which would mean that 'teaching to the test' would require imaginative teaching which reflected best practice. In this way the SATs could raise teaching standards.

The TGAT call for a simple structure was ignored and virtually all the subject Working Groups spawned multiple *Attainment Targets* (ATs) – science had 17, maths 14, geography began with 8. As if this was not bad enough, each AT was divided into *Statements of Attainment* (SoAs), intended as the building blocks or assessment criteria of a criterion-referenced assessment regime. By December 1990 the seven subjects on stream had between them over 1400 SoAs against which teachers would have to assess pupils (Stobart 1991). Primary teachers, who had to teach six of these subjects to large classes of pupils, were presented with an unmanageable assessment load.

What followed was a turbulent period of simplification (see Daugherty 1995 for a full blow-by-blow account) of the subject structures and the assessment regime, including the steady movement away from complex teacher-marked tasks to external tests.

What is important for our present purposes is how a criterion-referenced system failed to work. Some of the early tests attempted to target questions at a particular level (e.g. pupils would need to gain 7 out of the 10 marks on the Level 5 questions in order to get Level 5). This attempt at 'mastery' testing soon collapsed, as pupils were found to be failing at lower levels but then passing at one higher level – which was the level they received. After various complex experiments with alternative mastery-based scoring systems (see Massey 1995; Wiliam 1996), the approach has now switched to that of public examinations, in which the levels are fixed in relation to the total marks across the test – so that pupils get level 5 for being in the overall level 5 mark band, not because of their performance on the level 5 questions.

Similarly, teacher assessment has now moved away from extensive tick-lists and complex rules on how to aggregate Statements of Attainment to determine a pupil's national curriculum level, to a more holistic approach in which each level has a 'level description' and the teacher chooses which description 'best fits' the pupil's performance.

In relation to the use of criterion-referenced measurement, this movement away from detailed assessment, both in the externally set materials and in the requirements for teacher assessment, is instructive. What it demonstrates once again is the difficulty of defining complex tasks in a way that allows manageable and reliable assessment. Either the assessment must become more complex (for example, the driving test requires intensive one-to-one assessment) or the criteria must become more general and therefore less reliable, since differences in interpretation are bound to occur. This was compounded in the national curriculum by the nature of the SoAs, these having been written in order to define the curriculum and not as assessment criteria (Cresswell and Houston 1991). For example, the first SoA in level 9 Speaking and Listening (En1) in national curriculum English (1989 version) read:

> ❛ ... *give a presentation expressing a personal point of view on a complex subject persuasively, cogently and clearly, integrating talk with writing and other media where appropriate, and respond to the presentations of others.* ❜

In this form the SoA can hardly be regarded as usable as a means of criterion-referenced assessment: it would require a great deal of exemplification before any two teachers would be likely to interpret it in the same way.

Aggregation

The more complex and general the task, the more problematical producing a final grade or level becomes. This is particularly the case when, as in GCSE, A level examinations and (now) national curriculum end of key stage tests, 'compensation' is built in so that a poor performance in one part can be offset by a good performance elsewhere. In these mark-based approaches, low and high marks are combined to produce a 'middling' overall mark. Strict criterion-referencing does not work like this – pilots, for example, are expected to master every aspect of flying, and failure on one part leads to overall failure. It would be of little comfort to know that our pilot is extremely good at taking off and that this has compensated for poor landing skills. If strict criterion-referencing were translated into examination performance, it would mean that our grades would be determined by our *worst* skill areas; for example, if algebra was only grade F, then the overall grade for maths would have to be F; to give, say, an overall grade C despite the grade F, because geometry was grade A, would be misleading, because grade C level competence had not been shown in all areas of the subject.

Over-simplified measurement

The appeal of standardised tests and public examinations as the basis for comparing the performance of one school against another is an obvious one. The danger is that a summary statistic then becomes the accepted shorthand for making comparisons between schools or students. There may be all sorts of caveats and contextual information to go alongside the scores, but these are usually forgotten or discarded. House (1978), a leading American educationalist, described this trend:

> *There is a strong tendency for quantitative data to overwhelm other forms of information. Test scores are easy to feature in newspaper headlines and they have an appeal difficult to resist. The complex interpretations of what the data mean do not have the same persuasion nor lend themselves to similar exploitation by the mass-media.*

The most pervasive current form of this process are the government's *performance tables*, which provide summary statistics of GCSE and GCE examinations and, more controversially, various national curriculum key stage test results (see chapter 3). These allow parents to judge the relative performance of either the school (as with, for example, GCSE results) or the local education authority, as with the publication of Key Stage 1 results.

In line with House's remarks, the press have lost no time in taking the twelve columns of statistical information on schools' GCSE and GCE results – which include numbers of pupils with special needs and taking vocational qualifications – and putting them into rank order on just one variable: the percentage of students gaining five or more GCSEs at grade C or above. These *league tables* then allow easy comparison with other schools and with the national average.

A predictable response to this over-simplification is to illustrate the way in which schools have to operate under very different conditions, especially in terms of the attainments of the students who come to them at 11 or 13. A fairer system would be to take account of this and make some adjustment for it. This is the basis of the move to incorporate *value-added* measures – indicators which seek to show how much a school has increased pupils' attainment during their time there.

High-stakes assessment

What fuels the debates about league tables and value-added measures is that their repercussions for schools and colleges are substantial. At a time when funding follows pupils (i.e. schools and colleges are funded largely on the basis of the number of pupils/students they recruit), and in Further Education there is additional funding based on 'outcomes related performance' (i.e. for students who pass a qualification), it is vital to score well in the relevant league tables. This in turn puts pressure to do well in what is tested, which leads to 'teaching to the test'. In America such tests are called *high-stakes*. Because funding or recruitment rides directly on test scores, then the tests play a central role in determining the curriculum – what is tested is what is taught. We looked at the issues of Measurement Driven Instruction in chapter 1.

It is possible to monitor pupils' standards without resorting to high-stakes testing and the distortions to teaching and learning that may accompany it. In America, monitoring of national standards is done exclusively through *sampling* student performance rather than testing *all* students. In order to make reliable judgements on national performance, a carefully selected sample of 2500 students, out of a cohort of about 4 million, is sufficient to provide the necessary information on what students are achieving. These results are not used at the individual student level.

A good example of this strategy is found in the work of the Assessment of Performance Unit (APU) in England, which ran from 1974 to 1988. The APU supervised the national assessment of performance in maths, language, science, modern languages and design technology. Though initially set up to look at under-achievement, it soon became used by policy-makers and ministers as an indicator of educational standards (Gipps and Goldstein 1983).

What the APU did was to provide hard evidence of the levels of performance in various subjects. Because so few children in any school were used in the sample, schools did not feel threatened by the findings (i.e. it was not a high-stakes programme), which ensured the findings were likely to be accurate reflections of what pupils knew and could do. So when the Chairman of Jaguar Cars claimed that, of the young people applying for apprenticeship, a third *'couldn't even add up six plus nine'*, the Coventry education authority was able to report the APU findings that 94% of fifteen year olds could add two *four-digit* figures (*TES*, 16 May 1986). The same article reported the Minister of Technology as saying *'Schools are turning out dangerously high quotas of illiterate, innumerate, delinquent unemployables.'* The APU Language Team responded that *'No evidence of widespread illiteracy was discovered. On the contrary, the evidence is that most pupils have achieved a working literacy by the age of 11'* and *'no collapse of standards was discovered'*. The lessons here seem to be that we need systematic evidence to show typical standards at a given age – and even if we have it, some will choose to ignore it!

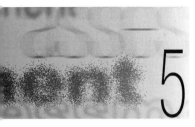

Fairness and equity in assessment

What is fair?

In this chapter we look at the complex issues of fairness and equity in assessment. We derive our use of equity from its legal meaning of *'the spirit of justice'*. We include a discussion of assessment in terms of equity in order to move beyond some of the more immediate concerns of fairness and bias. This is an area which has been under-developed in England, particularly in comparison with America where legal challenges have made it a critical issue in testing. We begin by looking at ways in which equity has been interpreted, especially in terms of **equal opportunities** and of **equality of outcome**. This leads to a discussion of forms of **bias** in testing. We follow this with some examples of group differences in performance and with our suggestions on how to ensure assessment practice is as fair as possible.

We saw in chapter 1 that one of the reasons formal examining was first introduced in England was to promote equal opportunities: the Civil Service examinations were introduced in the 1850s to permit advancement through talent rather than patronage. Just over 100 years later in the USA, however, this view was challenged. Tests and examinations were felt to be *denying* opportunities for advancement, particularly for black students. In the post-1965 Civil Rights legislation era, critics of 'advancement through testing' were pointing out that opportunities to acquire talent, or to be able to show it to sufficient effect in tests and examinations, were not equally distributed (Wood 1987). In other words, tests and examinations could be biased.

It is important to point out that both viewpoints may be advanced by the same individual. Thus, one might argue that public examinations are important as a means of equalising opportunities and as a necessary corrective to patronage, while at the same time understanding that tests and examinations may be biased in favour of one particular gender, social or ethnic group.

The argument in relation to IQ testing was examined by Mackintosh and Mascie-Taylor for the Swann Report:

> *Perhaps the most contentious assumption underlying the whole argument, however, is that IQ tests could ever provide a fair measure of the intelligence of children from working-class families, let alone those from ethnic or racial minorities.... If a child has been deprived of intellectual stimulation or educational opportunity, it is small wonder that his intellectual performance will reflect this fact. An IQ test is no more able to gauge a child's true innate potential regardless of the circumstances of his upbringing than is a pair of scales to measure his true potential weight regardless of what he has been fed.... To claim that IQ tests are biased is often only a way of making the point that IQ tests measure skills and knowledge which not all children may have been able to acquire; in other words, that differences in IQ scores are partly due to differences in the environmental experiences of different children.*
>
> (Mackintosh and Mascie-Taylor 1985, Annex D, Swann Report)

This quotation makes clear that there are two different issues at stake. Wood (1987) refers to these as *'the opportunity to acquire talent* and *the opportunity to show it to good effect'*. It is important to see the issues of unequal access to learning (the opportunity to acquire talent) and bias in assessment (the opportunity to show it to good effect) as separate.

Equity is not an underlying theme in education in England and Wales, and indeed there is little clarity about what it might mean. Debate and policy-making, where it has featured at all, has referred to **equal opportunities** in education, with a brief excursion into compensatory education for disadvantaged groups. Early attempts to achieve equality of opportunity, for girls and boys, focused in the main on equality of resources and access to curriculum offerings, particularly in science and maths. Important though this is, we now see it as a limited approach, given the very different out-of-school experiences of girls and boys. The fundamental problem is that this policy focus reflects a deficit model approach to inequality: girls are 'blamed' for behaving like girls and encouraged to behave more like boys. This model implies the possibility of overcoming disadvantage through the acquisition of what is lacking. This approach leaves the status quo essentially unchanged, since girls are unlikely to achieve parity through equality of resources and formal equality of access alone. As Yates (1985) puts it, *'where the criteria of success and the norms of teaching and curriculum are still defined in terms of the already dominant group, that group is always likely to remain one step ahead.'* Equal opportunities is a policy area which was hotly contested in the UK in the 1980s: seen by the extreme right as a revolutionary device which would disturb the 'natural' social order and as an attempt to attack White British society, and by the extreme left as essentially conservative because the gross disparities in wealth, power and status which characterise our society remain unchallenged.

A second approach is one which looks for **equality of outcome** (as evidence of equal opportunities), and this underpins analyses and discussions of group performance at public examination level in the UK. The attitude to equity in the USA is very different from that in the UK, for reasons of history and because of the population structure: *'The US has a long-term commitment to equity for its wholly immigrant population'* (Baker and O'Neil 1994) and is evidenced in equal outcome terms:

> ❛*The term* equity *is used principally to describe fair educational access for all students; more recent judicial interpretations, however, have begun the redefinition of equity to move toward the attainment of reasonably equal group outcomes ... the educational equity principle should result in students receiving comparable education yielding comparable performances.* ❜
>
> (Baker and O'Neil 1994, pp.11–12)

Our view, however, is that while one must strive to achieve *actual* equality of opportunity, equality of outcomes is not necessarily an appropriate goal: different groups may indeed have different qualities and abilities, and certainly experiences. Furthermore, manipulating test items and procedures in order to produce equal outcomes may be doing violence to the construct or skill being assessed and camouflaging genuine group differences (Gipps and Murphy 1994).

Apple's (1989) review of public policy in the USA, Britain, and Australia leads him to conclude that *equality* has been redefined: it is no longer linked to group oppression and disadvantage, but is concerned to ensure individual choice within a 'free market' perception of the educational community. In Apple's view, this redefinition has reinstated the disadvantage model and underachievement is once again the responsibility of the individual rather than the educational institution, or community. He argues that attention in the equity and education debate must be refocused on important curricular questions (to which we add assessment questions), as in Table 5.1.

Table 5.1 Curriculum and assessment questions in relation to equity (from Gipps and Murphy 1994, after Apple 1989)

Curricular questions	Assessment questions
Whose knowledge is taught?	What knowledge is assessed and equated with achievement?
Why is it taught in a particular way to this particular group?	Are the form, content and mode of assessment appropriate for different groups and individuals?
How do we enable the histories and cultures of people of colour, and of women, to be taught in responsible and responsive ways?	Is this range of cultural knowledge reflected in definitions of achievement? How does cultural knowledge mediate individuals' responses to assessment in ways which alter the construct being assessed?

To summarise our view: equity does not imply equality of outcomes and does not presume identical experiences for all; both of these are unrealistic. The concept of equity in assessment as used in this book implies that assessment practice and interpretation of results are fair and just for all groups.

Equity and assessment

Where does the debate about equity take us when it comes to assessment? It is important to remember that 'objective' assessment has traditionally been seen as an instrument of equity: the notion of the standardised test as a way of offering impartial assessment is of course a powerful one, though if equality of educational opportunity does not precede the test, then the 'fairness' of this approach is called into question. Most attainment tests and examinations are amenable to coaching, and pupils who have very different school experiences are not equally prepared to compete in the same test situation.

As Madaus (1992) points out:

> *In addressing the equity of alternative assessments in a high-stakes policy-driven exam system, policy must be crafted that creates first and foremost a level playing field for students and schools. Only then can the claim be made that a national examination system is an equitable technology for making decisions about individuals, schools or districts.*
>
> (p.32)

Bias

The non-technical notion of bias refers to *'prejudice'* or *'slant'*, although there are complex technical definitions in testing where bias is linked to validity (see chapter 4). The traditional psychometric approach to testing operates on the assumption that technical solutions can be found to solve problems of equity, with the emphasis on using elaborate techniques to eliminate biased items (Murphy 1990; Goldstein 1993). The limitation of this approach is that it does not look at the way in which the subject matter is defined (i.e. the overall domain from which test items are chosen), nor at the initial choice of items from the thus-defined pool; nor does it question what counts as achievement. It simply 'tinkers' with an established selection of items. Focusing on bias in tests, and statistical techniques for eliminating 'biased' items, not only confounds the construct being assessed, but has distracted attention from wider equity issues such as actual equality of access to learning, 'biased' curriculum, and inhibiting classroom practices.

There are two ways in which test developers can address bias. They look for:

▶ *item content bias*: **where there is bias perceived by users through examining the content;**

▶ *statistical item bias*: **where items or questions favour one or other group disproportionately (Smith and Whetton 1988). This is also called** *differential item functioning.*

Both of these 'biases' can be addressed during test development. The TGAT Report advocated looking for both sorts of bias, i.e. doing an item content 'sensitivity' review as well as a statistical analysis, when developing material for national assessment. In the USA this is now standard practice.

Item content bias would be detected by males and females and members of different ethnic groups reviewing items for gender bias, racial stereotypes or any material which could be offensive to a particular group. **Statistical item bias** is examined to determine whether any questions are disproportionately difficult for a particular group once that group's overall test performance has been taken into account. For example, *'car is to tyre as (tank) is to caterpillar'* was disproportionately easy for boys in one test, while *'dough is to pizza as (pastry) is to pie'* was disproportionately easy for girls (Smith and Whetton, *op cit*).

In America there is a *Code of Fair Testing Practices in Education* to which the major testing agencies subscribe. This requires them to indicate for all tests and assessments *'the nature of the evidence obtained concerning the appropriateness of each test for groups of different racial, ethnic or linguistic backgrounds . . .'* (JCTP 1988), and demands that *'Test developers should strive to make tests that are as fair as possible for test takers of different races, gender, ethnic backgrounds, or handicapping conditions.'* This has to be a step in the right direction. The code has nevertheless met with a certain amount of scepticism in America, largely because of the lack of any measures for enforcement. As a former Assistant Secretary of Education put it:

> **❛***If all the maxims are followed I have no doubt the overall quotient of goodness and virtue should be raised. Like Moses, the test-makers have laid down ten commandments they hope everyone will obey. That doesn't work very well in religion – adultery continues.* **❜**
>
> (*TES*, 25 November 1988)

However, there has been litigation over assessment in the USA, the most relevant being the suit the Golden Rule Insurance Company brought against Educational Testing Services (the equivalent of Britain's NFER), which develops insurance licensing examinations. The Golden Rule Company alleged that the test developed by ETS was discriminatory to blacks. The case was settled out of court in 1984 by an agreement, the key provision of which was that preference should be given in test construction to items that showed smaller differences in black and white performance. This has come to be called the Golden Rule Strategy, and the Golden Rule Bias Reduction Principle (Weiss 1987) states that *'among questions of equal difficulty and validity in each content area, questions which display the least differences in passing rates between majority and minority test takers should be used first'.*

Fairness and group differences

Bias in relation to assessment is generally taken to mean that the assessment is unfair to one particular group or another. This rather simple definition, however, belies the complexity of the underlying situation. Differential performance on a test – i.e. where different groups get different score levels – may not be the result of bias in the assessment; it may be due to real differences in performance among groups which may in turn be due to differing access to learning, or it may be due to real differences in the groups' attainments in the topic under consideration. The question of whether a test is biased or whether the group in question has a different underlying level of attainment is actually extremely difficult to answer.

When the existence of group differences in average performance on tests is taken to mean that the tests are biased, the assumption is that one group is *not* inherently less able than the other. However, the two groups may well have been subject to different environmental experiences or unequal access to the curriculum. This difference will be reflected in average test scores, but a test which reflects such unequal opportunity in its scores is not strictly speaking biased.

A considerable amount of effort over the years has gone into exploring cognitive deficits in girls in order to explain their poor performance on science tests; it was not until relatively recently that the question was asked whether the reliance on tasks and apparatus associated with middle-class white males could possibly have something to do with it. As Goldstein (1996) points out, tests are framed by the test developers' construct of the subject and their expectations of differential performance.

Of course pupils do not come to school with identical experiences and they do not have identical experiences at school. We cannot, therefore, expect assessment to have the same meaning for all pupils. What is important, though, is to have an equitable approach where the concerns, contexts and approaches of one group do not dominate. This, however, is by no means a simple task. For example, test developers are told that they should avoid any context which may be more familiar to males than females or to the dominant culture. But there are problems inherent in trying to *remove* context effects by doing away with passages that advantage males or females, because it reduces the amount of assessment material available. De-contextualised assessment is anyway not possible, and complex higher-order skills require drawing on complex domain knowledge.

What we can seek is the use, within any assessment programme, of a range of assessment tasks involving a variety of contexts, a range of modes within the assessment, and a range of response format and style. This broadening of approach is most likely to offer pupils alternative opportunities to demonstrate achievement if they are disadvantaged by any one particular assessment in the programme. Indeed, this is included in the *Criteria for Evaluation of Student Assessment Systems* by the USA National Forum on Assessment (NFA):

> ▶ **to ensure fairness, students should have multiple opportunities to meet standards and should be able to meet them in different ways;**
>
> ▶ **assessment information should be accompanied by information about access to the curriculum and about opportunities to meet the Standards;**
>
> ▶ **... assessment results should be one part of a system of multiple indicators of the quality of education. (NFA 1992, p.32)**

So far we have been addressing equity as a largely theoretical issue. For many teachers the most obvious practical expression is in differences of performance of boys and girls and between different ethnic groups.

Gender differences

In national assessment girls are outperforming boys in English and maths at ages 7, 11 and 14. In GCSE girls gain more higher grade passes (A*–C) than boys, a trend which has been growing since 1988. Since this coincides with the introduction of the GCSE, girls' superior performance was felt to be partly due to the style and approach of the new examination. Research shows, however, that coursework (see chapter 7) is not the main determinant of the final grade (Cresswell 1990; Stobart *et al* 1992). The GCSE examination did broaden the definition of achievement and the means of assessing it, while the introduction of the national curriculum meant that both genders had to study all subjects from 14 to 16, and it is likely that these two factors together have contributed to girls' growing success (Elwood 1995).

This pattern of performance has contributed to anxiety about the performance of boys in the UK.

❛*The failure of boys, and in particular white working-class boys, is one of the most disturbing problems we face within the whole education system.*

Girls outperform boys at 7, 11 and 14 in national curriculum assessments in English, maths and science. Girls are more successful than boys in almost all major subjects and are now achieving success in traditional boys' subjects such as design and technology, computer studies, mathematics and chemistry. Physics is the only subject in which boys now outperform girls. **9**

(Chris Woodhead, *The Times*, 6 March 1996)

A key factor is felt to be boys' lower motivation and more negative attitudes to school, particularly for working-class boys who can see reduced work opportunities for them in the changing labour market. Changing trends include growing part-time work, which women traditionally tend to take, and an increased service sector which requires high levels of communication skills, at which women tend to be better. However, two points need making here: first, that the boys who go on to GCE Advanced level do better than girls; and second, that gender, ethnic group and social class interact to affect performance.

At 18+, in the A level examination, boys gain more higher grades (A– C) than girls, even in subjects in which girls did particularly well at 16. For example, in English GCSE girls have 13% more high grades than boys, while at 18 boys have 3% more high grades than girls in English Literature A level, despite making up only 30% of the entry (Elwood and Comber 1996). Longitudinal analysis of pupil performance from 16 to 18 using a multi-level modelling technique shows that for boys and girls with the same GCSE score, girls make less progress to A level, gaining around two points fewer than equivalent boys (Goldstein *et al* 1997).

The research carried out by Patricia Murphy (1995) shows that girls and boys attend to different things in a task, and in this case neither response is wrong: both responses are valid, just different. But there is evidence that one reason for boys' poorer performance is that tests and examinations contain a greater verbal element than in the past, even in maths and science, and this is an area in which boys have always underperformed compared with girls. But also, she argues, there is evidence that boys tend not to use the sort of approaches to learning which current theories of learning advocate: relating knowledge to context in order to be able to apply it more widely; engaging in dialogue with other learners and the teacher in order to question and validate understanding; and using collaborative approaches to learning. These are some of the effective learning strategies which are more favoured by girls, and this may go some way to explaining recent patterns of boys' lower achievement. Therefore, boys' approaches to learning may need to be reconsidered and reconstructed (Murphy and Gipps 1996).

Things have come a long way since the days when young women were first admitted to examinations carried out by the London University Board. It insisted that they were chaperoned and, in case the length of the examination proved too much for them, drinks were served and buckets of cold water were available in case any of them fainted (Kingdon, quoted in Stobart *et al* 1992).

Ethnic group differences

A review of recent research on the achievement of ethnic minority pupils commissioned by OFSTED (Gillborn and Gipps 1996) showed that, since the previous major review of ethnic minority performance more than ten years previously (Swann 1985), there were generally higher levels of achievement, increasing year on year; improving levels of attainment among ethnic minority groups in many areas of the country; and dramatic increases in the examination performance of certain minority groups, even in LEAs where there is significant poverty. But the gap is growing between the highest and lowest achieving ethnic groups in many LEAs; African Caribbean young people, especially boys, have not shared equally in the increasing rates of achievement, in some areas their performance has actually worsened; and the sharp rise in the number of exclusions from school affects a disproportionately large number of black pupils.

Research on the performance of infant and junior school pupils does not paint a clear picture: on average, African Caribbean pupils appear to achieve less well than whites, although the situation is reversed in recent data from Birmingham. A more consistent pattern concerns the lower average attainments of Bangladeshi and Pakistani pupils in the early key stages, though this may reflect the significance of levels of fluency in English, which are strongly associated with performance at this stage.

There are no up-to-date nationally representative figures on GCSE performance by different ethnic groups. However, the review of research and new LEA data identified some common patterns. Indian pupils appear consistently to achieve more highly, on average, than pupils from other South Asian backgrounds. Indian pupils achieve higher average rates of success than their white counterparts in some (but not all) urban areas. There is no single pattern of achievement for Pakistani pupils, although they achieve less well than whites in many areas. Bangladeshi pupils are known on average to have less fluency in English, and to experience greater levels of poverty, than other South Asian groups. Their relative achievements are often less than those of other ethnic groups. In one London borough, however, dramatic improvements in performance have been made – here Bangladeshis are now the highest achieving of all major ethnic groups. African Caribbean pupils have not shared equally in the increasing rates of educational achievement: in many LEAs their average achievements are significantly lower than other groups. The achievements of African Caribbean young men are a particular cause for concern.

Tables 5.2 and 5.3 show how complex the patterns of performance are. Both are taken from the Youth Cohort Study, which is the only nationally representative data set to include information about class, gender and ethnic origin in England and Wales.

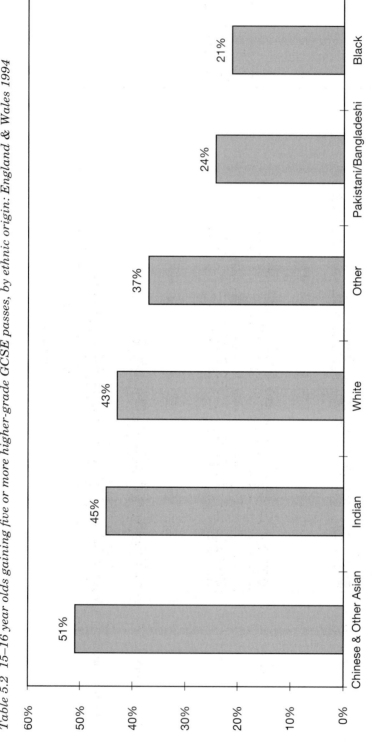

Table 5.2 15–16 year olds gaining five or more higher-grade GCSE passes, by ethnic origin: England & Wales 1994

Source: Youth Cohort Study of England and Wales, in Office for National Statistics (1996) Social Focus on Ethnic Minorities, London, HMSO

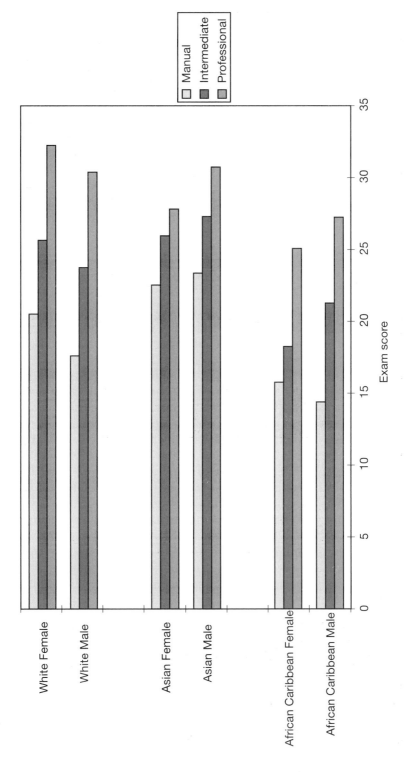

Table 5.3 Average exam score by ethnic origin, gender and social class: England & Wales 1985 (adapted from Drew and Gray 1990)

Table 5.2 shows the proportion of different ethnic groups gaining 5+ grades A–C at GCSE in 1994. Table 5.3, taken from Gillborn and Gipps (1996), shows average examination scores by ethnic group, gender and social class in 1985 (there is no more recent data containing all three factors). This table shows the complex interaction of social class, gender and ethnic origin: for example, only in the white group do girls consistently outscore boys, while among the Asian group that situation is reversed (although that pattern may have altered since 1985). Overall, the highest performing group is white girls from professional backgrounds and the lowest is African Caribbean males from a manual background.

Looking on the constructive side, work carried out at local education authority level indicates that where low-performing ethnic minority groups are targeted sensitively with additional educational resources, then those groups do perform at significantly higher levels (Gillborn and Gipps, *op cit*).

Towards fairness and equity

So how do we ensure that assessment practice and interpretation of results is as fair as possible for all groups? It is likely that a wide-ranging review of curriculum and syllabus content, teacher attitudes to boys and girls and minority ethnic groups, assessment mode and item format is required, as Table 5.1 shows, if we wish to make assessment as fair as possible. Although this is a major task, it is one which needs to be addressed, given the growing importance of standards, national assessment and public examinations.

We need to encourage clearer articulation of the test/examination developers' constructs on which the assessment is based, so that the construct validity may be examined by test takers and users. Test developers need to give a justification for inclusion of context and types of response mode in relation to the evidence we have about how this interacts with group differences and curriculum experience. The ethics of assessment demand that the constructs and assessment criteria are made available to pupils and teachers, and that a range of tasks and assessments be included in an assessment programme. These requirements are consonant with enhancing construct validity in any case. Given the detailed and, as yet, poorly understood effect of context on performance, the evidence that girls more than boys attend to context in an assessment task, and the ability of changes in the context of the task to alter the construct being assessed, the area of construct validity demands detailed study. We certainly need to define the context of an assessment task and the underlying constructs and make sure they reflect what is taught.

We also need to encourage the continued use of a range of assessment modes and task style; and to expand the range of indicators used: multiple indicators are essential, so that those who are disadvantaged on one assessment have an opportunity to offer alternative evidence of their expertise (Linn 1992).

If we wish pupils to do well in tests and exams, we need assessment which elicits an individual's best performance. This involves tasks that are concrete and within the experience of the pupil (an equal access issue), presented clearly (the pupil must understand what is required of her if she is to perform well), relevant to the current concerns of the pupil (to engender motivation and engagement), and in conditions that are not threatening (to reduce stress and enhance performance) (after Nuttall 1987).

Although we do not necessarily expect equality of outcome, we must continue to seek genuine equality of access; this means that all courses, subjects studied, examinations, etc., are actually equally available to all groups *and* are presented in such a way that all groups feel able to participate fully. One suggestion from the United States is that, since opportunity to learn is a key factor in performance, schools may have to '*certify delivery standards*' as part of a system for monitoring instructional experiences (Linn 1993). How realistic it is to do this remains to be seen, but it does put the onus on schools to address the issue of equal access, at an actual rather than formal level.

6 Assessment at primary level

The assessment issues at primary level are quite different from those at secondary level. Prior to national assessment, the emphasis had been on standardised tests rather than examinations, and the testing of basic skills – particularly reading – predominated.

The eleven-plus and after

The era of the eleven-plus was the heyday of the standardised test in primary schools. Not only did the examination itself contain a battery of tests, but children were prepared for it by taking tests regularly. The proportion of children going on to grammar schools was the criterion by which many parents and many teachers judged the 'success' of a primary school. Inside the primary school, the existence of the examination encouraged streaming and militated against mixed-ability teaching. It inhibited work on topics which engaged more than one skill and encouraged concentration on examination-type work, including practice in intelligence tests.

The demise of the eleven-plus, which began in 1965 with the introduction of comprehensive secondary schooling, had a significant effect on primary education in Britain. Freed from the constraints of a restrictive leaving examination, the curriculum opened out, different methods of grouping developed and styles of pedagogy changed. It was the era of the Plowden Report (and a certain amount of hype) and suddenly British primary schools practising discovery-learning and integrated, cross-curricular and child-focused teaching were world famous. Although not all that was written about British primary schools in the 1970s was true, there is no doubt that changes took place and that primary education did broaden and open out. None of this could have happened if the eleven-plus had still been in existence.

What also happened, around 1978, was that many local education authorities re-introduced standardised testing programmes. Circular 10/65, which heralded the introduction of comprehensive schools, had been followed by a dramatic drop in attainment testing by LEAs, but in 1975 and 1977 came the Black Papers with a concern over standards of teaching and learning, and in 1976 James Callaghan, then Prime Minister, made his Ruskin College speech demanding more accountability in education. At this point many LEAs, concerned that they had no information on standards of performance in their primary schools, brought back reading, maths and to a lesser extent reasoning tests. However, this testing was of little significance: results were not published, there was no competition among schools to do well, there was little link with the curriculum taught and little effect on children's life chances. It was 'low-stakes' assessment, with the results collected routinely for administrative purposes and as a safety net for the LEA. Thus, by contrast with the eleven-plus, these tests had little impact on teaching, and their introduction took place alongside the continued expansion of teaching methods and organisation.

After the era of the eleven-plus, assessment at primary level was very much for professional purposes: for feedback on teaching, identifying children with special needs or delays in learning, and for record-keeping: while assessment at secondary level continued to be dominated by the selection and certification functions of public examinations at 16 and 18.

Raising standards and expectations

Concern about standards in education in recent times began to be voiced in 1976 with the speech given at Ruskin College by the then Labour Prime Minister, James Callaghan. In it he argued that curriculum, standards and accountability of schools were issues of national importance which should be open to debate. The Green Paper *Education in Schools: A Consultative Document* (DES 1977) which followed it had a major section entitled 'Standards and Assessment'. In this, the case for *'a coherent and soundly based means of assessment for the education system, for schools, and for individual pupils'* (p.16) was argued. However, the efforts of the Conservative government in the following decade focused on reforming the examination system at 16+ to give a unified GCSE, relying on the work of the Assessment of Performance Unit (APU), HMI and public examinations to give a picture of national standards (Daugherty 1995). The 1977 Green Paper, issued by a Labour government, had rejected the regular testing of all pupils in basic skills, national monitoring of standards, and performance tables enabling parents and the public to compare schools. Within ten years these were explicitly to be part of the policy of the Conservative government. The detailed political and policy argument which took place during those ten years is well described by both Daugherty (1995) and Ball (1990).

The 1985 White Paper *Better Schools* (DES 1985), issued by Sir Keith Joseph, concentrated on raising standards and contained the first suggestion that national attainment targets, accompanied by some form of national assessment, should be introduced into the final years of primary school, to parallel the national criteria which had been introduced for the new GCSE. (See also Gipps *et al* 1995.)

In autumn 1986 a new education minister, Kenneth Baker, was appointed. He announced the decision to impose a national curriculum in January 1987 and outlined plans for the national curriculum and accompanying national assessment in April that year. These resulted in the publication of *The National Curriculum 5–16: A Consultation Document* (DES 1987a), which described in general terms a national curriculum backed by clear assessment standards which would form part of an Education Bill to be introduced later the same year. In this document the following claim about assessment and raising standards was made:

> ❛ 7 ... *Pupils should be entitled to the same opportunities wherever they go to school, and standards of attainment must be raised throughout England and Wales.*
>
> 8 *A national curriculum backed by clear assessment arrangements will help to raise standards of attainment by*
>
> (i) *ensuring that all pupils study a broad and balanced range of subjects. ...*
>
> (ii) *setting clear objectives for what children over the full range of ability should be able to achieve. ...*
>
> (iv) *checking on progress towards those objectives and performance achieved at various stages, so that pupils can be stretched further when they are doing well and given more help when they are not. ...*
>
> 23 *Attainment targets will be set for all three core subjects of mathematics, English and science. This is a proven and essential way towards raising standards of achievement. Targets must be sufficiently specific for pupils, teachers, parents and others to have a clear idea of what is expected, and to provide a sound basis for assessment.* ❜

(DES 1987: 3–4, 9.10)

It is important to look at the link between testing and raising standards in education, the implicit belief being that introducing an assessment programme will *ipso facto* raise standards. The publication of examination results has, since 1980, been seen as one way of *maintaining* standards. We know that the imposition of assessments or examinations which are very important for either pupils or teachers will have a direct effect on what and how teachers teach (see also chapter 1) but, as we will investigate in more detail later, it is important not to have too simplistic a model of how this operates.

National curriculum assessment

The national assessment programme, as outlined in the Report of the Task Group on Assessment and Testing (DES 1988) and the statutory Orders, required that pupils be assessed on a ten-level scale against the attainment targets (ATs) by their teachers and at the ages of 7, 11, 14 and 16 by external tests (originally called standard assessment tasks or SATs). At these ages, the results of ATs were combined and reported towards the end of that school year. At other ages, assessments were recorded but not necessarily reported, except to parents.

The series of ten levels (now reduced to eight) was designed to enable pupils to demonstrate progression: most pupils of 7+ are expected to be at level 2 in the system, while most pupils of 11+ are expected to be at level 4.

The first run of assessments for 7 year olds in English, maths and science took place in 1991, with the second run in 1992. By 1993, the scope of the assessment programme and the time it took had been dramatically reduced, but many schools, as a result of a national boycott organised by the three largest teacher unions, either did not carry out the testing or did not report the results to their local education authorities. In 1994 the boycott continued, but by 1995 all schools were carrying out national assessment at the end of Key Stages 1 *and* 2.

Changes since 1994

The teachers' boycott of national assessment led to the Review of the National Curriculum and Assessment by Sir Ron Dearing. After the Review, the following changes were made at age 7: league tables were dropped; testing of science was dropped, although teacher assessment continued; tests for spelling continued; a new number test was introduced in 1994, and a reading comprehension test in 1995. At age 11 the first full testing took place in 1995 (with the tests externally marked to reduce the load on teachers); mental arithmetic tests were introduced in 1997; there is a spelling/handwriting test as well as two tests in each of English, maths and science. The standard tests are paper-and-pencil exercises, very far from the original activity-based standard assessment tasks advocated by TGAT, although children at Level 1 and below still take SATs in small groups. The myriad Statements of Attainment were replaced by fewer, broad Level Descriptions; teachers were advised to get rid of 'tick charts' for recording progress and make 'best fit' judgements for teacher assessment. Teacher assessment is reported alongside the test results, to give it parity of esteem, although moderation was made non-statutory from 1994 (for a detailed account, see Clarke 1996).

At the end of Key Stage 1, the procedure in outline is as follows: during the spring and early summer term of the year in which pupils reach the age of 7 (Year 2), teachers make a Teacher Assessment (TA) of each pupil's level of attainment using levels 1–4 of the scale in relation to all the attainment targets of the core subjects. Teachers may make these assessments in any way they wish, but observation, regular informal assessment and keeping examples of work, are all encouraged. In the first half of the summer term the pupils are given, by their teacher, a series of standard assessment tasks or standard tests in English and mathematics. For pupils aged 11 (Year 6), a series of national tests is administered in May covering English, mathematics and science.

The NAPS study

A number of researchers have reported on the introduction of the national assessment programme at primary level (Bennett *et al* 1991; Pollard *et al* 1994; Gipps *et al* 1992). In this chapter we will draw heavily on the evaluation/research carried out by the National Assessment in Primary Schools[2] (NAPS) project from 1990 to 1996 and the discussions found in Gipps *et al* (1995). This research focused on teachers' assessment practice and how this changed and developed as a result of the national assessment programme.

Research on assessment in primary schools in the early 1980s (Gipps *et al* 1983) had shown that teachers' understanding of issues in assessment was very limited: while there was widespread use of standardised tests of reading and maths, there was little understanding of how the scores were derived, or what they meant, and no understanding of issues such as reliability and validity. Their own assessments were intuitive and discursive, rather than against criteria, and often not written down; teachers found it hard to articulate their assessment practice. The NAPS research set out to see what happened to primary teachers' assessment practice when they were faced with the demands of national assessment; with little training and few materials, how did these teachers carry out the hundreds of teacher assessments required of them? How did they manage the standard assessment tasks (SATs) and what did 'standard' mean in this setting? Given the legal requirements to assess, coupled with the very high profile that came with reporting to parents and the publication of league tables, how did teachers react? Did they become 'technicians' administering external tests (as they were in the early 1980s) or did they engage with the issues and become skilled assessors?

[2]ESRC Refs: R00023 2192 & 4438

Key Stage 1 (assessment at age 7)

Key Stage 1 assessment began in 1991. Increased levels of discussions and collegiality were observed in our schools in the early stages of the implementation: from teachers of other ages to support Year 2 teachers who, it was felt, were faced with an awesome task; and among Year 2 teachers throughout the study to negotiate meanings for SoAs and standardise judgements. Heads' involvement supporting their staff meant that there was a feeling of *'being in it together'* which also helped to develop collegial ways of working. Helping each other with SATs and moderating SATs and TA brought teachers out of their classrooms and into working contact with each other.

One theme which the researchers first came across in 1991 (Gipps *et al* 1992) was the raised professionalism of Year 2 teachers; this was reported in a third of our schools and involved Year 2 teachers' leading assessment training and policy development. By 1994 five of the eleven primary headteachers who were left from the original study (having continued through to the second stage of our research looking at Key Stage 2) stressed the contribution their Year 2 teachers were making to assessment at Key Stage 2.

Raising standards

In only the second year of national assessment the government was able to show that standards had risen: the then Secretary of State for Education, John Patten, held a press conference at the end of 1992 proclaiming raised standards, since the percentage of the 7-year-old population reaching higher levels had risen in reading, spelling and maths (*Seven year olds' results show improving standards*, DFEE press release, 21 December 1992). Patten took this as evidence that the national curriculum was 'working'. From this study we would say that this rise in levels of performance was due to teachers teaching more of what was required in the SATs: punctuation, spelling, handwriting and mental arithmetic. There was more attention to 'the basics' in 1992 and 1993, and this showed up in the children's improved levels of performance. The experience of doing the SATs also helped teachers to understand the assessment criteria, so they could teach in a more focused way in later years. Of course, given the changes in the curriculum and to the assessment tasks in each of the three years, together with the lack of dependability of results (Shorrocks *et al* 1992), such changes in patterns of performance should be treated with caution.

What the NAPS teachers were doing was not generally teaching directly to specific test items (although children were doing 'quick' mental arithmetic in order to be able to do sums in the test within five seconds), but teaching areas of the curriculum so that their children could do assessments on those topics. The difference between this situation and that in other countries, where teaching to the test is observed, is that in England and Wales we have an imposed curriculum as well as imposed testing. There is, therefore, *something other than tested items for teachers to teach towards*. In addition, the assessment tasks have changed each year and there has been a rolling programme of attainment targets included in the testing, so teachers cannot easily become too narrow in preparing pupils for the tests. These are important positive considerations in response to Madaus' critique of Measurement Driven Instruction (see chapter 1).

The NAPS teachers did find criterion-referenced assessment difficult in the early stages: in 1991 and 1992, many found it difficult to evaluate the children's attainment and award a level *without* giving any recognition to factors such as behaviour, effort and progress. Some teachers were adamant that with young children such assessment was inappropriate and interfered with the teachers' attempts to maintain motivation and self-esteem. In aggregating results to provide a final grade for public examinations, compensation – setting a good performance in one area against a poor performance in another – is usually allowed, thus reducing the strictness of the criterion-referencing. This, however, is not the same issue that our teachers were facing: whether and how to allow 'compensation' for progress and effort.

What the NAPS study showed clearly was a shift in infant teachers' assessment practice (notwithstanding individual variation) from an intuitive approach to one based on evidence and written records. Also, it is clear that the bulk of our teachers became more knowledgeable in assessment, rather than merely being technicians operating an imposed system (see Gipps *et al* 1995 for a detailed account).

Best performance

The research indicated that there are specific issues related to the age of the children being assessed which mean that they require a particular type of assessment programme. For example, our teachers commonly tried to get the best performance out of the children by reassuring them, helping them, offering preparation and emotional support and sometimes even a second chance. Developments in educational assessment suggest that one aspect of a good assessment is that it elicits best performance (Wood 1986; Nuttall 1987; Gipps 1994) and that this adds to the test's validity. The evidence from the NAPS study was that teachers tried in the assessment programme to elicit best performance from the pupils on the SATs, through encouragement, offering good conditions, etc. This was probably not due to teachers' particular models of assessment, but rather to their view of what is appropriate for children of this age. Teachers were concerned about 'failure' and 'labelling' for such young children, and there was some tension between offering children the chance to try the next advanced level in the assessment programme, or indeed to keep plugging away at a particular assessment task, and the need to prevent the children experiencing failure.

A number of other studies of national curriculum assessment at both 7 and 14 (SEAC 1991) indicate that the SAT, with its emphasis on active, multi-mode assessment and detailed interaction between teacher and pupil, may, despite the heavy reliance on language, provide a better opportunity for many children. This is particularly the case for minority and special educational needs children, as it allows more opportunities for them to demonstrate what they know and can do than traditional, formal tests with limited instructions; in other words, they elicited best performance. The key aspects seem to be:

▶ **a range of activities, offering a wide opportunity to perform;**

▶ **match to classroom practice;**

▶ **extended interaction between pupil and teacher to explain the task;**

▶ **a normal classroom setting, which is therefore not unduly threatening;**

▶ **a range of response modes other than written.**

To conclude, we see that as a result of the national curriculum and assessment programme, teachers of 7 year olds have redirected the focus of their teaching and this has been reflected in improved national assessment results in the 'basic skills'. Greater care in planning, close observation of children and a more detailed understanding of individual progress impacting on teaching were reported by over half our headteachers, as well as a lasting effect on collaboration and discussion by a smaller number. The SATs have acted as a training device, and group moderation has broken down barriers.

This came about, however, not because of having to give an external standardised test (as with Year 6 teachers and the Key Stage 2 testing in 1994), but because of the demands of teacher assessment and the performance-type activities in the SATs. It was these requirements which, together with the (albeit too detailed) specification of the curriculum, had in headteachers' views led to an improvement in planning, teaching and assessing in Year 2 classes. We do not intend to downplay the problems in the assessment programme, for there were many (overload; too many and yet inadequate assessment criteria; low levels of training, particularly for TA; undependability of the results, etc), but to make the point that if we wish to raise real standards of teaching and formative assessment (which in turn supports teaching and learning) then we need more than imposed external traditional tests.

Key Stage 2 (assessment at age 11)

Key Stage 2 testing is at an earlier stage of introduction: it began in earnest in 1995. The assessments are, for the most part, standardised tests not assessment tasks. It was always planned to put results into league tables, hence one might predict a fairly substantial teaching-to-the-test impact.

The impact of Key Stage 2 testing has already been directly observable. In 1995, thirty-two schools which had been involved in piloting Key Stage 2 tests since 1993 reported that, as an outcome, they had changed their forms of organisation:

▶ **fourteen had changed from mixed-ability teaching to some form of setting;**

▶ **eight had moved away from cross-curricular topic work towards more subject-based teaching;**

▶ **fourteen heads had introduced regular formal testing throughout the whole key stage;**

▶ **the tests had also made an impact on teaching – for example, a greater focus on reading and spelling, and presenting maths in a way that children are more likely to meet in the test papers;**

▶ **in addition, *all* the teachers involved had done something to prepare their pupils for tests – for example, revision in science, past papers in maths, timed tests in English.**

We also found, however, that teachers had in many cases changed their *teaching style*. We interviewed 29 Key Stage 2 teachers in depth about their teaching approach in 1995. Fifteen out of the 29 teachers reported different teaching modes for different circumstances. They described when they would become chiefly *'transmitters'* of knowledge and when they would encourage children to discover for themselves and when they felt they were *'constructing learning together'*. These would change in relation to teaching different subject areas; teaching different children; teaching different age groups; using different forms of pupil organisation; and school ethos. None of the teachers endorsed the 'transmission' approach to teaching on its own; similarly, few rejected it outright – they limited this approach to certain purposes.

That half our sample explicitly espoused the mixed-mode approach to teaching is interesting in the light of our teachers' more general comments on the effect of the national curriculum on their teaching practice. Although not one teacher believed that children learn solely from the transmission of facts, one-quarter felt pushed into doing more of this because of the amount of work to be covered by the national curriculum, or in some cases by the tests. They also felt unable to use children's ideas as starting points for work, and regretted this. Examples of their comments were:

> **❝**[Considering the model] *the teacher conveys information to children and that is how learning takes place – I think that is the way I almost felt pushed to go by the weight of the curriculum.* **❞**

6*the teacher conveying information to children – I think that has come much more to the fore with the NC, simply because of the volume of content that we have to deliver.* 9

6*What I think ... I suppose it's quite child-centred, isn't it? What I think and what the Government think are two completely different things. If I think how I was teaching five years ago, and how I'm teaching now. There always was input from me, but probably more and more now because there is so much to be got through.* 9

Conclusions

Through both key stages we can discern quite clearly a teaching-to-the-test effect; because the curriculum is broad and assessment of the 'process' skills is required through teacher assessment, this effect is not so far particularly negative or narrowing. Although many teachers regret the loss of autonomy, the national curriculum and assessment programme has served to bring practice across schools closer, which may well be desirable in a national system. As Clarke (1996) argues about impact:

6*Lauren and Daniel Resnick laid down three principles for accountability assessments, based on their analysis which revealed that 'measurement driven instruction' will lead reform in the wrong direction if the tests embody incomplete or low-level learning goals.*

1. You get what you assess *('If we put many multiple-choice tests into the testing system, we must expect children to practise answering multiple-choice questions. In contrast, if we put debates, discussions, essays and problem solving into the testing system, children will spend time practising those activities').*

2. You do not get what you do not assess *('What does not appear on tests tends to disappear from classrooms in time').*

3. Build assessments toward which you want educators to teach *('Assessments must be designed so that when teachers do the natural thing – that is, prepare their students to perform well – they will exercise the kinds of abilities and develop the kinds of skills and knowledge that are the real goals of educational reform').* 9

The effects on Key Stage 2 teachers' assessment skills has been less marked so far than for Key Stage 1 teachers; this is due, we suggest, to the reduced requirements for teacher assessment and the standardised nature of the tests. By contrast, because of the high stakes there has been more effect on organisational and teaching practice in order to achieve high results.

Baseline assessment

In September 1996 SCAA issued a consultation document on baseline assessment – the assessment of children on entry to reception classes in infant schools. Such early assessment was widely carried out before this date, with SCAA (1996) reporting that around half of all LEAs in England were involved in baseline assessment schemes. The value of such early assessment is that it provides vital diagnostic information for the teacher: it is a classic form of formative assessment, as the teacher adjusts her schedule for the child who does/does not know his or her colours, numbers or letters. The Secretary of State felt that, given the importance of such assessment, it should be more consistent:

> *These assessments vary enormously in their origin, format, content and style. Some schemes involve teachers writing descriptive comments or ticking criteria in a checklist, with the children being largely unaware of being assessed. Others involve teachers in assessing children as they work with them. Some schemes requiring one-to-one or small-group assessments take a considerable amount of classroom time. Some schemes focus entirely on the basic skills of literacy and numeracy, whilst others assess across a broader range of areas of learning, often including aspects of personal and social development. The extent to which parents, pre-school providers and other adults in the classroom such as classroom assistants contribute to the assessments also varies considerably.*

(SCAA 1996, p.4)

SCAA was therefore asked to undertake a consultation exercise and develop a national framework for baseline assessment. At the time of writing, this framework is not yet finalised, but local schemes will be accredited by SCAA and there will also be a national model. All schemes should assess language and literacy, mathematics and personal and social development; assessment should take place within seven weeks of starting school; and take no more than 20 minutes per child (a pretty tall order, given the scope!).

An important function of such assessment is also, of course, to provide a baseline for value-added measures of school performance, and in the current climate this is why baseline assessment has been so widely endorsed. However, as chapters 3 and 4 show, there are a number of caveats to the value-added, performance table debate.

Value-added analyses will be turned by hook or by crook into league tables, and because league tables are irresistible they will become public. We would argue that value-added analyses at age 7 will be harmful, not helpful, because the assessment will then become 'high-stakes' at 5 as well as 7, with all that implies for pressure on teachers and children, teaching to the test, etc. Of course, at age 7 it will be interesting and important to look back and see what progress has been made by the individual and within the school, but our view is that these children are too young and vulnerable to be used as tools of accountability.

We need to be absolutely clear about the role that this development is to play. Assessment in a 'low stakes' or relaxed environment is rarely harmful; and assessing children on entry to school is important, so that teachers know what children can and cannot do. It is the use to which the results are put that is crucial to the impact that assessment has. Assessment at this age should be for supporting the learning and teaching of the child; assessment information should therefore be used within the teacher–parent–school triangle.

In any case, assessment at this age is not likely to be sufficiently 'reliable' to be used for high-stakes purposes. Value-added analyses at age 11 come soon enough, particularly if the purpose is to monitor the performance of individual primary schools, and can be calculated on the basis of the 7-year-old scores, once both sets of assessments settle down and become sufficiently reliable for these analyses (see also Gipps 1997).

7 Assessment at secondary level

Secondary school assessment is construed as taking examinations: the Key Stage 3 tests at 14, GCSE at 16 and A levels or GNVQs at 18. We therefore begin with a reminder that this view underplays the key role of the teacher's informal and formative assessment of pupil work in learning – assessment *for* learning (chapter 2). Crooks' evaluation of how teacher assessment influences learning suggested four main ways: providing motivation (success in the subject and self-confidence in the learner); deciding what to learn; helping students learn how to learn (effective learning strategies); and helping students judge the effectiveness of their learning. All these effects are at work in the primary school, as we saw in the previous chapter. The transfer to secondary school, with its emphasis on subject disciplines taught by different teachers, raises the issue of the impact of assessment in the different culture of the secondary school or, later, in the Further Education or Sixth Form college.

What seems clear is that while the majority apply themselves, with varying degrees of enthusiasm, to their secondary school courses, there is a significant proportion of pupils who either become disaffected with schooling and/or who cannot meet the demands of the curriculum. Sir Ron Dearing's *Review of 16–19 Qualifications* was driven in part by the 'long tail' of underachievement in the secondary school population in England. In terms of both motivation and achievements this is particularly a problem for boys. We acknowledge the difficulties teachers face in dealing with pupils who do not see education as important or as any kind of passport to success. The issue is how to make learning an active and successful experience for all (see the National Commission on Education's 1995 *Success Against the Odds* for a constructive treatment).

Though much of this chapter will be focused on summative assessment, we want to emphasise that effective learning takes place largely as a result of skilful informal assessment, through clear articulation of standards and expectations, and through feedback and encouragement, rather than through the 'carrot and stick' of examinations, the knowledge for which is often quickly forgotten.

Using assessment information at transfer

Pupils arrive at secondary school with an educational history, much of which is to do with assessment. This is self-evident, but what is much less clear is what use is made of it by the receiving school. The general pattern seems to be 'hardly any'. Research before the advent of national curriculum assessment showed that most primary schools used published tests, the results from which were passed on to the secondary school but not used. Teachers were reluctant to make use of the tests diagnostically or to adjust the curriculum in the light of what the results showed (Gipps *et al* 1983). One claim from secondary teachers whose schools took in pupils from large numbers of feeder schools has been that the data were too varied to be useful. In theory, national curriculum assessment should generate standard information for such schools, as the Key Stage 2 results provide both teacher assessment and national test results.

In 1995 a research study tracked the way transfer data was being used in 21 secondary schools (McCallum 1996). The main purpose for this information, often accompanied by discussion with the feeder school, was to create balanced tutor groups – *'who goes with whom and who should be separated from whom'*. National curriculum assessment results were added to a mass of information which included ticklists of the curriculum covered, samples of work, reading test scores and Record of Achievement folders. The research showed that no consistent use was made of what was given. Once the tutor groups had been formed, the material was 'passed on', but there was little consistency as to which members of staff had access to it. McCallum concludes:

> **❝**The situation seems to have progressed little since the 1980s, because of:
>
> - *the actual use made of assessment information in Year 7;*
>
> - *the reluctance of teachers to prejudge children;*
>
> - *the perceived unreliability of TA and SAT results;*
>
> - *the variety of formats in which the information appears.* **❞**
>
> (*op cit*, pp.13–14)

This is a longstanding and unsatisfactory state of affairs. It suggests that there is little acceptance of other teachers' assessments, which in turn fuels the resentment of primary schools who have passed on detailed findings which are promptly ignored. It leads to secondary schools adopting a 'clean-slate' approach and then spending time and money testing new arrivals on tests.

A radical solution to this would be to follow the example of France and move the national testing to the *start* of secondary schooling rather than have it at the end of primary (Broadfoot 1996b). This means a change of purpose, the tests becoming essentially diagnostic (but also offering a value-added baseline measure). They would, however, no longer serve the purpose of evaluating primary school performance. This makes better assessment sense, but in the current 'accountability' climate we may be whistling in the wind.

A less dramatic solution is for secondary schools to design their own transfer sheets so that they collect data they will use. We maintain that the 'clean slate' approach to assessment information is an abdication of professional responsibility rather than the adoption of an altruistic position towards providing a fresh start for the pupil (who will be tested anyway to establish attainment levels). Using primary school data may also lessen the dip in pupils' performance when they start secondary school, since it should reduce 'hit-and-miss' setting of expectations and levels of demand.

Key Stage 3 assessment

The national assessment of pupils at 14 has been one of the bloodiest battlegrounds of national curriculum implementation. We will review the main action relevant to assessment issues. Daugherty (1995) provides a full, blow-by-blow account of the skirmishes up to 1994.

The Key Stage 3 curriculum was first introduced, in science and mathematics, in 1989, with English following in 1990. This key stage covers three years (Years 7–9) and therefore the first full end-of-stage assessment would have been in 1992. During this period there was considerable controversy about the form of the end-of-stage assessment, one which mirrored much of the Key Stage 1 debate over length, complexity and teacher assessment. The development agencies, following the logic of the TGAT report, produced lengthy classroom-based Standard Assessment Tasks (SATs), one of the English ones taking some six weeks for pupils to complete (see Gipps 1992, for details of these approaches). In 1991, a new Secretary of Education, Kenneth Clarke, undermined the pilot work by describing it as *'elaborate nonsense'* and announcing:

> **❝**I am persuaded that the process will be more manageable and the results will command more confidence if the tests are mainly in the form of short written tests. **❞**
>
> (Daugherty 1995, p.53)

1992 therefore saw the piloting of short written tests in English, mathematics and science. In contrast to Scotland, where protests took the form of parents refusing to send children to school on test days, there were record attendance figures for Year 9 pupils. These teacher-marked tests attempted to use a criterion-referenced approach, which gave rise to a variety of anomalies (e.g. pupils passing at a higher level having failed at a lower one – see chapter 4). This pilot year was merely the lull before the storm. In 1993 the tests, by then largely developed by examination boards, were disrupted by teacher boycotts. While work-load was the legal basis for the boycott, the real cause had been teachers' objections to the English tests – both their content and the threat to publish national results even though the tests had not been adequately trialled. In this conflict the intransigence of John Patten, as Secretary of State for Education, meant he became one of its casualties.

The first step to getting teachers back on board was to relieve them of the marking burden, and a further revision of the national curriculum – the third for English and fourth for Design & Technology since 1988. In 1995 the tests were externally marked and the papers sent back to the schools. The result of this move was an outcry, again from English teachers, objecting to the severity of the mark scheme and marking which led to over 80,000 pupils' results being contested.

The 1996 Key Stage 3 tests were therefore the first 'settled' testing of the full 14-year-old cohort. What is significant for our purposes is that by this stage they were essentially conventional examinations. Pupils expected to be at levels 3–7 are entered for two test papers which take 2–3 hours in total. These are externally marked and level boundaries are set for the total marks after reviewing the candidates' performance. Students wanting the level 8, now the top level on the scale, must take an extra extension paper of $1-1\frac{1}{2}$ hours. Pupils at levels 1–2 are assessed through standard tasks rather than the tests. There is teacher assessment across the curriculum for all pupils, and this is reported separately alongside the test results. All this seems a long way from the lofty hopes of the TGAT report which initiated national curriculum assessment.

Given the discussion of validity in chapter 4 it is worth considering how the results will be used. At present, schools have to report to parents their child's score alongside the scores for the school and the national averages. In 1996, 57% were at level 5 (the expected level for a 14 year old) or above in English, 56% in science and in mathematics. The similarity of these distributions is intriguing, as will be the discussion of whether or not standards are improving should these percentages fluctuate.

GCSE

The introduction in 1988 of the GCSE as the national examination for 16 year olds in England, Wales and Northern Ireland (Scotland had its own Standard Grade) was in many ways a politically remarkable event. This was because it was introduced by a Conservative government which was willing to replace the cherished GCE O level and the Certificate of Secondary Education (CSE) with a single examination which incorporated features of both (see Kingdon and Stobart 1988 for a detailed account).

As a new and therefore unfamiliar examination, GCSE proved

remarkably successful. At the heart of this success has been the introduction of more imaginative and flexible syllabuses and assessment techniques, not least the introduction of **coursework**. Indeed, in the first few years of GCSE students were so motivated by the prospect of coursework counting towards the final grade (which it rarely did with O levels) that there was evidence of students over-working as they sought to meet similar deadlines in each of their eight or more subjects (Kingdon and Stobart 1988). GCSE English, for which most students followed 100% coursework syllabuses, proved particularly demanding. This pressure was subsequently reduced by more tightly defined requirements – for example specifying the maximum number of words required, and by government limits on the proportion of coursework.

Differentiation

Because GCSE was expected to be taken by virtually all pupils, assessment techniques were required which could handle such a broad range of achievement. The approach adopted involved **differentiation** and **positive achievement**. A differentiated examination is one in which *'different components are deliberately set at different levels of difficulty to meet the needs of candidates with different levels of ability'* (*GCSE General Criteria*, 1985). In the second edition of this book we discussed in some detail the various models that were available ('three-in-line'; four overlapping papers; extension papers) as these were largely unfamiliar. We have since become familiar with *tiered papers* and *extension papers* in national curriculum assessment. In GCSE, differentiated papers have now been extended to subjects as diverse as psychology, business studies and design & technology.

POSITIVE ACHIEVEMENT
Part of the rationale for differentiation is that it allows students of all attainment levels to show *positive achievement*. The intention here is that papers can be set that allow candidates to demonstrate what they *'know, understand and can do'*. Thus, rather than taking an examination paper which becomes a dispiriting experience for students at the lower grades, it becomes a constructive experience.

MOTIVATIONAL ISSUES
This approach does raise motivational and policy issues: in any differentiated papers scheme, a decision must be made about the tier at which to enter a student; this in turn affects motivation. For example, students on the lowest maths tier can gain a maximum of grade D, irrespective of how well they perform. It can be argued that they would have been entered for the most appropriate tier by their teachers. However, there is some cautionary evidence of students being wrongly entered –

either failing because they were entered for too high a tier and 'falling off' by not achieving the minimum grade, or by being put in for too low a tier and getting a restricted top grade (e.g. grade D).

There was startling evidence of the former in the first year of GCSE maths, when over 38000 students who were entered for the top tier (grades A–D) came away with no grade (U = Unclassified). Some of this wrong entry was put down to pressure from parents who would not agree to entering their child for a tier with a maximum of grade C. Subsequent research also showed that a proportion of students were entered for the middle tier, with a ceiling of grade C, whose work would have merited a grade B (IGRC 1992). There was a high proportion of girls in this group, suggesting that teachers had lower expectations of their achievement in maths. Further studies confirmed that there were teacher assumptions that girls would not be able to handle 'exam pressure' – though a review of their examination performance found no evidence of this (Stobart *et al* 1992). The findings led to SCAA modifying the way in which tiers overlap in order to prevent this kind of distortion. However, there was still evidence from subjects using tiered papers for the first time in 1996 (such as Psychology and Sociology) that choosing the appropriate tier remains a problem for a significant proportion of students.

MEASUREMENT ISSUES

Differentiation has also brought its share of measurement issues, not least whether the same grade gained by different routes is comparable. For example, students can get a grade C on either the intermediate tier (which offers G–C) or on the higher tier (D–A*). What research has consistently shown is that it is easier to get a C on the lower tier than on the higher. This finding is sufficiently robust to have been dubbed the *Good & Cresswell Effect* after the researchers who first identified and explored it (Good and Cresswell 1988). Even where there has been a common paper – or, as at present, some common questions on separate papers – awarders still appear to be harder on candidates who take the harder route. The explanation for this seems to be largely psychological: examiners expect more from candidates on the harder route, even from those who gain the lower grades, than from those who score highly on easier papers and are given the equivalent grade. This phenomenon can in turn lead to cynical 'easier option' entry policies by teachers and students for whom a grade C is critical for league table and selection purposes – a negative effect of high-stakes testing.

Not all subjects have differentiated papers. Whether they have or not is determined by SCAA. The alternative is **differentiation by outcome**, in which students take the same papers and it is their responses which differentiate. GCSE Art provides an example: all students do the same work, but the range of responses provides sufficient differentiation (or *'discrimination'* as it is technically, but unhelpfully, known) to award the full range of grades. Interestingly, GCSE religious studies and history have common papers, with history marking schemes based on 'levels of response', whilst geography, home economics and most other subjects have differentiated papers.

GCSE comparability

The issue of whether, within the same GCSE, one route to a grade C is easier than another, is just one example of several comparability issues within GCSE. The fact that in 1997 there were six examining groups each offering several different examinations in the same subjects indicates the scale of the problem facing those who need to ensure that grades are comparable. This is then compounded by concerns addressed in chapter 3 about comparability over time: *Is my grade C this year the same as yours last year?* We consider comparability later in this chapter in connection with A levels – for which the issues are the same but the stakes higher.

GNVQ Part One

As the restrictions on GCSE coursework and syllabuses begin to produce a standard form of GCSE assessment, increasing numbers of 14–16-year-old students are being given an opportunity to experience a different approach. The Part One GNVQ (an unhelpful title, given there is not a Part Two) is the result of Sir Ron Dearing's recommendation to provide 14–16-year-old students with a vocational 'taster'. This led to the development of Part One GNVQs, qualifications with three vocational units and three 'key skills' units which are equivalent to two GCSEs. The Part One pilot began in 1995 and by September 1997 there were over 400 schools taking seven subjects.

Chapter 8 provides more detail on GNVQs but the salient point here is that the Part One provides some variety to the assessment diet. The qualification is modular and is essentially coursework-based. Students are given prespecified outcomes and are expected to work independently to gather evidence, as well as working in groups on assignments.

Early feedback suggests this has not only motivated some students who have previously shown little interest in GCSE courses, but has caused teachers to re-evaluate their teaching style, giving an emphasis to active and independent learning. One teacher reported a 14 year old approaching her and saying *'You're not going to talk much today are you, Miss, 'cos I've got work to do.'*

The future of GCSE

We believe that the earlier, less constrained, GCSE met many of the requirements of a 'good' examination in that there was a mix of coursework and examination (determined by 'fitness for purpose'); it encouraged teachers to be innovative and respected professional judgements; it motivated students through coursework, and through more imaginative syllabuses than those of the GCE it replaced. The politically imposed limits on coursework (the personal wish of John Major) have weakened the model, as may the reduction of syllabuses and teacher freedom.

There are those who see the idea of major public examinations at 16 as an anachronism. As one of the few remaining industrialised nations where compulsory schooling ends at 16 rather than 18 years of age, the GCSE is seen as a block on moving to a coherent 14–19 policy. Proponents of abolition are generally looking for a modular 'credit' framework which would allow students to take a mix of academic and vocational courses which would take students seamlessly through to work or higher education. Once again Scotland is likely to lead the way. There, the *Higher Still* proposals have already led to the merging of vocational and academic qualifications and a credit framework.

The other source of opposition to the GCSE are those who see that the use of GCSE results primarily for league tables is leading to negative rather than positive effects. David Hart, general secretary of the National Association of Head Teachers, brings together both arguments:

> *The current system, tied to league tables, is producing a concentration on those capable of achieving 5 or more A–C grades, and is causing real problems for the lower achievers – although, as a country, we have recognised that we need to take urgent and effective action to help these people. . . . The GCSE also militates against the idea of a coherent 14 to 19 curriculum. The NAHT has long doubted the value of GCSE as an exam at 16-plus, particularly with the introduction of the national curriculum and major reforms taking place at 17-plus and 18.*

('Heads seek death of "stifling" GCSE', *TES*, 23 August 1996)

GCE Advanced level

Anyone trying to understand the education system of England, Wales and Northern Ireland soon learns of the key role of GCE A levels. The A level is pivotal to university admission and, as an examination which has only changed incrementally since it was introduced in 1951, is familiar. This conservatism is understandable: just about every policy-maker, editor, politician and professor of education has A levels, has prospered, and is paying (in one way or another) for children to do the same. Thus when all around is changing (GCSE, GNVQ, etc), there is comfort in this stability: the merest hint that A level might be changed leads to talk of *'debasing the academic gold standard'* (*Daily Telegraph* editorial, 10 April 1996).

A more detached look, however, leads to some critical questions:

▶ **Is the narrowness of taking two or three subjects, usually in related areas, appropriate as the basis for twenty-first-century, lifelong learning?**

▶ **Given that grade points are the basis for university entrance, are the grades reliable?**

It was these questions that Sir Ron Dearing addressed in his *Review of Qualifications for 16–19 Year Olds* (1996). We will look at what he proposed, and the reactions to it, as this may well provide the development agenda for the next few years.

The Dearing Review

The Dearing *Review of Qualifications for 16–19 Year Olds* did not simply cover GCE A level but looked at the full spectrum of qualifications for 16–19 year olds. This leaves us with a national system of thousands of qualifications, dominated by A levels which most educationalists and employers see as too narrow and academic. This over-specialism is of particular concern when other countries – particularly those enjoying greater economic prosperity – require a much broader general education for 16–18 year olds.

It was this mix of over-provision and over-specialism which led to the remit given to Sir Ron Dearing in his *Review of Qualifications for 16–19 Year Olds*, which was published in March 1996. In the case of A levels, the remit was *'to maintain the rigour of GCE A levels'*.

Dearing's dilemma was therefore to reform the system without changing the central features. The aim was to provide a system of qualifications which will be competitive with other nations (who currently lead us in meeting National Targets) and which will provide students, including the disaffected, with suitable qualifications.

Proposals

The Dearing Review ran to 600 pages and 198 recommendations, which may explain why it was so well received by all parties – it had something for everybody: more rigour; more breadth; more status for vocational qualifications; more key skills. The *Daily Telegraph* wryly commented: *'any initiative that receives a unanimous welcome in so contentious a field as education should set alarm bells ringing'* (28 March 1996).

Dearing does not attempt to bring together the three pathways, the academic, the applied (e.g. GNVQ) and the vocational (e.g. the work-related NVQ), into a single route – the more radical option favoured by many. Instead he recommends a national framework for qualifications which would operate at four levels: **entry**, **foundation**, **intermediate** and **advanced**. National qualifications would be allocated to the appropriate level: for example, GCSE grades A*–C would be at intermediate level, grades D–G and NVQ Level 1 at foundation level. The innovation here is the entry level, which is intended for students performing below GCSE. It will be graded A–C, which corresponds to national curriculum levels 1–3. (See Table 7.1)

Table 7.1 Dearing's proposed framework for national awards

National Award: ADVANCED LEVEL		
AS and A Level	GNVQ Advanced Level	NVQ Level 3
National Award: INTERMEDIATE LEVEL		
GCSE Grades A–C	GNVQ Intermediate Level	NVQ Level 2
National Award: FOUNDATION LEVEL		
GCSE Grades D–G	GNVQ Foundation Level	NVQ Level 1
National Award: ENTRY LEVEL		
Common to all pathways: three grades A/B/C		

One of the intentions of this approach is to emphasise the equivalence of the three 16–19 pathways – academic, applied and vocational – each of which will be represented in the three higher levels. It will also give employers an indication of the demand of particular courses as they will have a level 'badge' to accompany them.

Breadth

While this framework may begin to bring more coherence to those qualifications which have been allocated to a national level, it does not in itself deal with the narrow specialism of the 16–19 curriculum of many students. In particular it does not address the absence of key skills (previously known as core skills and a compulsory part of GNVQs) as part of A level. Dearing addresses this by proposing **National Certificates** – see Tables 7.2 and 7.3.

Table 7.2 Intermediate Level National Certificate

Five GCSEs Grade C or above, including English, Maths, IT (full or short course)	GNVQ Intermediate (includes key skills)	Full NVQ Level 2 plus key skills level 2 (either GCSE grade C in English, Maths, IT or NCVQ key skills units)

Table 7.3 Advanced Level National Certificate

Two GCE A levels plus key skills (level 3 NCVQ units or key skills AS)	GNVQ Advanced (includes key skills)	Full NVQ Level 3 plus level 3 NCVQ key skills or key skills AS

At the intermediate level this would involve five GCSEs at grade C or above, including English, mathematics and information technology, or an intermediate GNVQ (which includes the key skills) or a NVQ level 2 plus the key skills/GCSE equivalent.

At advanced level it would involve two A levels, or a full GNVQ at Advanced level or a full NVQ at level 3 plus competence in communication, the application of number and information technology demonstrated through NCVQ key skills units at level 3 or through a new AS level in key skills (see below).

Dearing recognises that this falls short of the breadth of study called for by supporters of a Baccalaureate-style qualification. He therefore proposes the creation of a **National Advanced Diploma** which would involve four areas of study: sciences; arts & humanities; modern languages; and the way the community works – for example, business. This would involve study to at least the new Advanced Subsidiary (AS) standard or of units from other GNVQ or NVQ subjects.

Additions such as this could lead to the charge of making the system even more complicated. Dearing therefore offsets this by proposals to slim down what is already on offer – particularly the multiplicity of A level syllabuses – and to standardise language and processes. Central to this is the bringing together of the two regulatory bodies, SCAA and NCVQ, as the Qualifications and Curriculum Authority (QCA) from 1 October 1997, coupled with suggestions for further mergers between vocational and academic examining bodies.

The key criticism of this approach is its voluntary nature. Unless university selectors require at least a National Certificate, it seems unlikely that it will gain any currency. The proposal for a broader based Diploma has also run into traditionalist opposition. *The Times* lead editorial commented: *'this runs counter to the spirit of specialism that makes the A level system so attractively rigorous'* ('The A level should not be debased', 28 March 1996). More ominous is the fact that the major school and college teacher organisations have joined together to pronounce that it is *'too prescriptive, discriminates against scientists and would only serve an academic elite'*.

Introducing the new AS

Dearing recognised that the GCE A levels, because of their public standing, *'has led to their expansion beyond the purposes for which they were created'*. Better options are needed for students who cannot meet their demands. The current Advanced Supplementary examination, intended to be at full A level standard but half the size, is acknowledged to have been an unsuccessful approach. In its place Dearing proposes a new (but long-campaigned for) qualification – the Advanced Subsidiary. This will provide a middle step between GCSE and A levels and would make demands appropriate to the first year of the sixth form. Again the intention is to offer more breadth in the curriculum and to give opportunities to those who may be unable to meet the demands of the full A level. The key assessment issue is how a new 'standard', equivalent to the first year of A levels, is to be created so that it is both reliable and comparable across subjects. This is likely to be a process based on examiner-judgement rather than on statistical techniques (see Cresswell 1996).

One of the most far-reaching proposals was for the introduction of a **key skills AS**. The key skills (formerly known as core skills) are compulsory units in the GNVQ. Strong pressure from employers that communication, application of number and information technology should be a compulsory part of the 16–19 curriculum ran into problems with A level. It was argued that this would add an additional burden to students, many of whom were having difficulty meeting the demands of A levels. The solution is a separate qualification, with both examinations and coursework, which covers the three skills. The incentive to take this would be to make it a requirement for the National Certificate and to encourage universities to require it for entry.

Subsequent consultation did not support a separate key skills AS. The preference is to use the NCVQ key skills units and to provide assessment based on four levels rather than GCE grades.

Maintaining A level rigour

Rigour is one of the report's key words. Interpretation becomes critical, given that – like virtue – nobody would oppose it. The remit to 'maintain the rigour of . . . A levels' leaves little room for manoeuvre when dealing with a 45-year-old qualification which, in terms of progression, is probably the most 'high-stakes' qualification in the land – success or failure at A level has far more implications than gaining a degree. Dearing's logic is that if other, more suitable qualifications are being introduced for the bulk of students, then the rigour of A levels can be further increased. This will come in the form of adjusting the grading of those subjects judged to be relatively lenient (such as art, design & technology, home economics, classical studies and English). The justification for this is set out in the *Quality and rigour in A Level examinations* background paper. For the most able students there will be a revived emphasis on additional 'Special Papers', which have been teetering on the verge of extinction over the past decade. In addition, such students may be encouraged to take university modules while still at school and subsequently to get recognition for this.

Not all have welcomed this as the way forward, including Eric Macfarlane, a former FE college principal:

> *Sir Ron has responded with a set of proposals to make A levels less flexible and accessible.... One suspects that it will be the additional academic options that will be given priority by those currently following the academic route. This will be a big step backwards. The proposed AS half-subjects and S-level papers were both features of the Higher School Certificate. By the end of the century the sixth-form curriculum of the public schools and a reintroduced selective system looks like being indistinguishable from that of 50 years ago.*
>
> ('Sir Ron and the great however', *TES*, 12 April 1996)

The greatest concern for the rigour of A levels comes from a recent, powerful and relatively unnoticed change: the move to **modular syllabuses**. Over half the current A level syllabuses are modular and the uptake has been dramatic, particularly in mathematics. The benefits of modularity, particularly in relation to student motivation, are acknowledged. However, modular syllabuses can be seen as a threat to the maintenance of standards on two main grounds: *'the absence of the major challenge ... [of] ... a final examination of all the skills, knowledge and understanding achieved during the whole programme'* and the availability of resits which allow students to improve their grades. The Report recommends that resits should be limited, that there should be a final 'synoptic' examination worth at least 30% of the total mark (and with at least half those marks for questions on the syllabus as a whole). Consideration should also be given to having a modular first year and a conventional 'linear' second year of A level.

Subsequent tightening by SCAA of the regulations for modular A levels will mean that modules can only be re-taken once, and immediately the final synoptic module is taken the final grade will be awarded (i.e. there is no re-take of this module). Even this has not satisfied leader writers, who see modularity as a weakening of standards. *The Times* thundered:

❛*Modular teaching is the enemy of excellence and a hidden danger in an ever-more competitive world. Sir Ron should not be giving it any encouragement. The A level is the qualification to which pupils aspire and which employers respect. Specialist knowledge, sophisticated skills and tough final examinations are its hallmarks. The Government should get back to these basics.* ❜

(28 March 1996)

This seems ironic given the extent to which modular courses are an accepted part of university degrees. The discussion of whether modular approaches compartmentalise learning and restrict the integration of knowledge is, though, a legitimate one. It raises the issue, discussed in chapter 2, of the kind of learning we want. Are conventional A level examinations tougher because they require much more recall or because they call for deep learning which is not found in module examinations? What evidence is there that students taking conventional ('linear') A levels do integrate their knowledge across the topics or domains that are separately examined?

Comparability

Much of the discussion concerning rigour revolves around whether subjects, syllabuses and assessment schemes are equally demanding. This is essentially an issue of reliability (see chapter 4). The perception is that, with six examining boards offering over 600 syllabuses, comparable standards may be difficult to guarantee. The same is true at GCSE. A particular concern is that some subjects appear easier (i.e. give more higher grades or give higher grades to students with weaker GCSE results than in other subjects), a problem when university entry may be decided on total grade points.

At the heart of the concern for comparability is the prospect that students could be disadvantaged because they took a subject, or a syllabus within a subject, which made it more difficult for them to get the same grades as equivalent students taking different subjects or a different syllabus in the same subjects. In England, and to a lesser extent in Wales and Northern Ireland, this problem has been accentuated by the number of examination boards offering the same qualifications. Because these are commercial organisations (even though they have charitable status and have been traditionally linked to universities), their aim has been to meet market needs. This has meant that each board has also offered a variety of syllabuses within the larger-entry subjects. While there has been a steady process of merging examination boards and reducing the number of syllabuses, there is still enormous variety within the system. In 1996, 1110 GCSE and 487 GCE syllabuses were examined by the boards.

Given the high-stakes nature of GCE and GCSE grades, the relatively small-scale comparability exercises which the boards jointly undertake (22 between 1985 and 1996) do little to convince doubters that the standards of one board are the same as any other. Most teachers will have a view on the relative demands of the different boards and syllabuses within these boards.

A more drastic solution has therefore been proposed: reduce the number of examination boards and syllabuses. This would reduce variability and allow SCAA to monitor examination performance more effectively through its system of assessors (who attend and are active in award meetings) and its scrutiny programme, which monitors examination board compliance with the Codes of Practice for GCE and GCSE. The outcome of this is that each examining board is to be allowed only two syllabuses in major subjects – defined at A level as having an entry of 15000 or more – and one (possibly shared) in smaller subjects. Thus the current 600+ syllabuses will drop to around 200, including the new AS. In addition, subjects will have to include the revised subject cores to ensure substantial overlap of content.

In 1996–97 the Secretary of State for Education, Gillian Shephard, demanded a reduction of examining boards and vocational awarding bodies. At the time of writing there are plans for three 'unitary' examination boards in England which offer GCSE, GCE and vocational qualifications. In Scotland, the Scottish Qualifications Authority offers both academic and vocational qualifications.

The dilemma for this drive towards reliability, which constrains both content and assessment, is how to guarantee that syllabuses will develop and change in order to meet changing needs. Much of the previous curricular innovation launched new styles of examination (e.g. Nuffield Science, Schools Council History, Avery Hill Geography) which in turn became mainstream syllabuses. Under the current restrictions, what will persuade an examining board to drop an established syllabus in order to take on a more experimental one?

Another concern echoes those of our treatment of Measurement Driven Instruction in chapter 1. Will one syllabus produce an arid teaching approach, based no doubt on a best-selling textbook, which has students skilfully rehearsed for the test but leaves them with little love of the subject?

The changes to Key Stage 3 and to public examinations at 16 and 18 demonstrate yet again that when assessment is high-stakes, either in terms of selection or of monitoring institutional performance, the emphasis shifts to the *reliability* and *comparability* of qualifications. The cost may be in terms of imaginative teaching and effective learning. If motivation is based primarily on getting good results, then what kind of learning will our students come away with? T. H. Huxley captured this nicely in his 1874 university address: '*[students] work to pass, not to know; and outraged science takes her revenge. They do pass, and they don't know*' (Bibby 1959).

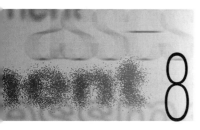

Assessing vocational qualifications

8

One of the most surprising statistics in Sir Ron Dearing's *Review of Qualifications for 16–19 Year Olds* was the estimate that there are over 16000 qualifications available for this age group. The vast majority of these are vocational qualifications, and these courses can range from one-day training to three years full-time. In 1996–97 over 5700 courses, operated by over 130 awarding bodies, received government funding. These figures are a useful reminder that most teachers will only encounter the tip of the iceberg and that the assessment issues raised by vocational qualifications are often overlooked.

We have used *vocational* in its most general sense to cover both school- and college-based courses which introduce students to relatively large occupational sectors (e.g. GNVQ Leisure & Tourism) and occupational courses which assume the candidate is working in that sector (e.g. NVQ Hairdressing). It is these highly specific occupational qualifications which provide the bulk of the qualifications available to 16–19 year olds.

Given the relative unfamiliarity of vocational qualifications to many teachers, we provide some examples of what a typical NVQ and GNVQ look like as well as discussing the assessment issues they raise. We have chosen these examples because they are central to government efforts to rationalise vocational qualifications – and already over one million NVQs have been awarded. The majority of qualifications still remain outside this framework at present, but we are likely to see increasing convergence. We also return to the issues of criterion-referencing, competency, mastery-learning and reliability which we introduced in chapter 4.

Competency-based occupational qualifications

The appeal of competency-based qualifications in the workplace is that they demonstrate that the candidate is able to perform the tasks explicitly required for the qualification. We want our airline pilots to have practical competence in all aspects of flying a plane, not higher degrees in astrophysics. Qualifications based on guilds and apprenticeship have a long and respectable pedigree. Given the diversity of these awards, the problem has become one of their recognition and currency in a world where jobs change rapidly and 'guild knowledge' will no longer secure a lifetime's work.

In order to try to bring the jungle of occupational qualifications into some sort of order, the government has encouraged a framework of vocational qualifications. In England, Wales and Northern Ireland this was the task of the National Council of Vocational Qualifications (NCVQ), established in the mid-1980s, with Scotland having its own Scottish Vocational Educational Council (SCOTVEC). The result was a system of National Vocational Qualifications (NVQs, or SVQs in Scotland) which operated at five levels across eleven 'framework areas'. The levels move from level 1 – *'competence which involves the application of knowledge in the performance of a range of varied work activities, most of which may be routine and predictable' (NCVQ Data News, Spring 1997)* to level 5 – *'competence which involves the application of a significant range of fundamental principles across a wide and often unpredictable variety of contexts. Very substantial personal autonomy and often significant responsibility for the work of others and for the allocation of substantial resources feature strongly. . . .' (op cit).* The framework areas cover wide sectors of employment. The first, for example, is 'Tending animals, plants and land' and within this are qualifications as exotic as Fish Husbandry (Shellfish) and Amenity Horticulture (Sportsturf Maintenance).

Each NVQ is developed by a **lead body** which represents the occupational area and which develops the requirements by means of a *functional analysis* of what knowledge and what competencies are required at each level at which the qualification will be offered. These **standards**, as the specifications are called, are then approved by NCVQ or SCOTVEC (later the Scottish Qualification Authority). Assessment is conducted through approved awarding bodies such as City & Guilds, BTEC and RSA, though there are several hundred smaller awarding bodies.

NVQ assessment

Our particular concerns are with the assessment issues which NVQs raise – of which there has been no shortage. Many of these relate to our discussion of criterion-referencing in chapter 4. NVQs are structured as modular qualifications in which units, which may vary in size, are further divided into **elements** – for example *'Obtain information from an established storage system'* (Level 2 Business Competence). The outcomes needed to demonstrate this will be made explicit in **performance criteria** – for example, *'required information is promptly located, obtained and passed to correct person or location'.* The contexts in which this would be expected to be performed are further defined through **range statements** and there may also be further amplification of the knowledge and understanding required. Assessment of this competence is most likely to be through the visit of an individual assessor, who will confirm that the tasks have been covered and recorded and who may either see demonstrations or question candidates about their understanding.

The main practical criticism of NVQ assessment is that it involves copious amounts of paperwork, often of the tickbox variety, which almost becomes more important than the competencies being recorded. This problem conceals a more fundamental issue: how can standards be presented so that they are unambiguous to the candidate and the assessor? The route the NVQ has taken is, as we saw in chapter 4, the one which national curriculum assessment originally took and which the GCSE grade criteria fleetingly attempted: *to increase clarity by ever tighter definition of what was required*. All this was done in the faith that clear and unambiguous standards could be written. Alison Wolf has been consistently critical of this belief:

> ❛*this ever receding goal of total clarity derives not from bad luck or incompetence, but is actually inherent in the methodology adopted. The more serious and rigorous the attempts to specify the domain being assessed, the narrower and narrower the domain itself becomes, without, in fact, becoming fully transparent. The attempt to map out free-standing content and standards leads, time and time again, to a never ending spiral of specification.* ❜
>
> (Wolf 1995, p.55)

The solution for Wolf, which runs parallel to the changes to national curriculum assessment, is to accept that assessment should be kept relatively simple and general, and must be complemented by networks of assessors and exemplar materials plus '*a good deal of realism about what can be claimed and achieved*' (*op cit*).

A second major criticism of the NVQ approach relates to the role of knowledge and theory in a 'can-do' qualification. Alan Smithers has taken a high-profile role in this criticism, which includes unfavourable comparison with European vocational education:

> ❛*It has been assumed that if students can show themselves capable of carrying out specified tasks, the necessary knowledge and understanding must have been acquired and need not be separately assessed. . . . Similarly, because of the disregard amounting to disdain for 'knowledge', there are no conventional written examinations.* ❜
>
> (Smithers 1993, p.9)

While these criticisms are far from accurate (there are examinations in some NVQs, many specify the knowledge required) there is widespread agreement in educational circles with this position, though employers seem less concerned about these points.

The response to these criticisms was for DFEE to set up an independent review of the 'top 100' NVQs, headed by Gordon Beaumont. The report, published early in 1996, was critical of their complexity and confusing jargon. It recommended a simplified structure to the written standards which must be written in 'plain English'. They should be accompanied by exemplars and guidance, more emphasis should be placed on external assessment and all assessment methods should be approved by NCVQ. These findings are being implemented from 1997.

General vocational qualifications

The assumption underlying the more general vocational qualifications is that they prepare students **for** employment, and/or further study, rather than develop their competency **in** work. They are likely to be taught in schools and colleges as full-time courses, though often work experience is encouraged. GNVQ and BTEC Nationals are probably the most familiar examples. There is also a range of more specific and practical courses such as Pitman's typing and secretarial qualifications which are seen as a pre-work qualification.

The General National Vocational Qualification (GNVQ)

We will go into some detail about the GNVQ, because it is a qualification that most teachers have heard of, but know relatively little about.

GNVQ is a vocationally oriented qualification which was introduced in 1992 and is offered in schools and colleges by three awarding bodies (BTEC, City & Guilds and RSA). It owes much of its current structure and terminology to NVQ, from which it was derived. It currently operates at three levels – Foundation; Intermediate; Advanced – and has over 200,000 16+ students on courses. The qualification is modular and essentially coursework-based, with students graded (pass, merit, or distinction) on their 'portfolio of evidence'. Currently fourteen subjects are offered, the most popular being Business, Health & Social Care, Leisure & Tourism and Art & Design.

At **Foundation** level students take three common mandatory units (including a test on each) plus three optional units. In addition, three 'key skills' (formerly core skills) units in communication, application of number and IT have to be passed at level one. The qualification is equivalent to four GCSEs at grades D–G. The structure of the **Intermediate** level is four mandatory units, typically with three tested, and two optional units. The three key skills have to be passed at level two and the qualification is equivalent to four GCSEs at grades A–C. Students taking the **Advanced** GNVQ have to complete twelve vocational units, eight of them mandatory (with typically seven tested), and the three key skills units at level 3. All this is equivalent to at least two GCE A levels.

UNIT STRUCTURE

There is a common structure to all GNVQ units. This involves specifying what the student should achieve (*performance criteria*), defining what this should cover (*range*), and suggesting how this should be presented (*evidence indicators*). There is then supplementary guidance (*amplification and guidance; teachers' notes*). Table 8.1 provides an example of this structure.

UNIT CONTENT

The emphasis of the GNVQ is on *application* of vocational knowledge, understanding and skills. Each qualification therefore incorporates applied elements – for example seeing how an actual industry/business works, organising an event. This content derives from collaborative work with both the occupational sector and teachers. The mandatory units have been produced by NCVQ and are common for all awarding bodies.

ASSESSMENT

At all GNVQ levels, a pass is awarded to students when they are assessed by their teacher as having met all of the performance criteria and evidence indicators for the vocational units (each of which may contain up to twenty performance criteria and six evidence indicators), have passed the external tests, and have shown evidence of covering the key skills at the appropriate level. In order to award merit and distinction grades, teachers must judge whether students have met three 'process' themes (planning; information seeking & handling; evaluation) and a 'quality of outcomes' theme in at least one-third of the portfolio. The difference between merit and distinction resides in the complexity of the assessment activities, the independence of the students' approach and the depth of knowledge and understanding in their response. The emphasis on independent learning is therefore reflected in the grading criteria. Similarly the key skills are intended to encourage competence in communication skills (particularly spoken), handling of numerical data and information technology.

Before a school or college can offer a GNVQ it must meet agreed **centre approval criteria**. These involve making sure the centre has sufficient resources and expertise to offer the qualification. One of the guidelines is that teachers (*assessors*) are trained or training on the appropriate NVQ assessment and verification units (*D32–33*) or the GNVQ Planning and Assessment units.

The external checks on the teacher assessment come in the form of **internal** and **external verification**. The former operates within the centre and involves a qualified assessor making sure assessments are consistent.

Table 8.1   Example of an Element (Intermediate Business, Unit 3)

Element 3.4: Present proposals for improvements to customer service

PERFORMANCE CRITERIA

A student must:
1. explain the **importance of customer service** in business organisations
2. identify **how business** organisations **monitor customer satisfaction**
3. identify **improvements to customer service**
4. present proposals for **improvements to customer service** in one organisation

RANGE

Importance of customer service: to gain and retain customers, to gain customer satisfaction, customer loyalty, to enhance organisation's image

How businesses monitor customer satisfaction: numbers of customers, level of sales, feedback (repeat business, complaints), marketing research

Improvements to customer service: reliability, friendliness, availability of goods or services, speed of delivery, published policy for exchanges or refunds, access to buildings (wheelchairs, pushchairs), care for the environment (rubbish-free, clean), customer safety

EVIDENCE INDICATORS

A record of a presentation proposing improvements to customer services in a business organisation. The presentation should show how improvements could help attract customers, secure customer satisfaction and customer loyalty, and enhance the organisation's image. The presentation should include examples of improvements to three of the following: friendliness, availability of goods or services, speed of delivery, policies for exchanges or refunds, access to buildings (wheelchairs, pushchairs), customer safety and care for the environment.

Notes to support the presentation describing customer services in one business organisation, stating how the organisation monitors its customers' satisfaction and outlining proposals for improvement to customer service.

AMPLIFICATION

Numbers of customers (PC2 range) a measure of customers as observed by students. They are not expected to access statistical information.

Level of sales (PC2 range) a measure of the up-take of goods or services as observed by students. They are not expected to access statistical information. Sales can be as diverse as 'signing up for a college course' or 'buying a pint of milk'.

Feedback (repeat business, complaints) (PC2 range) information gathered formally and informally.

Marketing research (PC2 range) information gathered in a structured way from a targeted audience to provide a business with specific information about customer satisfaction.

The external verifier is appointed by the awarding body and visits the centre at least twice a year to review a sample of portfolios and confirm the standard of the work.

A further external check is the tests, which are intended to confirm the students' coverage of the subject content. These tests are machine-marked and have a pass mark of 70%. They are offered three time a year at present. They are not graded.

PART ONE GNVQ
One recommendation of Dearing's review of the national curriculum was that students at Key Stage 4 (14–16 years) should have an opportunity for a 'vocational taster'. For this, the Part One GNVQ was developed. Because the current Intermediate and Foundation GNVQs are full-time courses, the Part One uses three, rather than six, units plus the three key skills units to provide a two-year course equivalent to two GCSEs. A pilot, jointly operated by SCAA and NCVQ, has been running since 1995 and over 400 schools and 10000 pupils are currently involved. The qualification anticipated some of the subsequent changes to the full GNVQ by adding tests which contribute to the final grade ('extension tests') and introducing 'controlled assignments' to help standardise teacher assessment.

Assessment issues in GNVQ

While in theory criterion-referenced assessment is welcomed for making transparent what is required, in practice this clarity is elusive – as we saw with NVQs. In the summer of 1995 John Capey (Principal of Exeter College) was asked by NCVQ to lead an independent review of GNVQ assessment. His review found consistent criticism from teachers, students and the inspection agencies about the burden and reliability of the assessment system. Many of the positive benefits of GNVQ were being offset by laborious assessment and paperwork requirements to check whether all the detailed range statements had been covered. In addition, the complex grading criteria meant many teachers made a second scan of the portfolio, to identify the process skills (planning, information seeking, evaluation) and high quality outcomes – and demonstrated little confidence that they could apply the criteria reliably. Ensuring *coverage* of key skills also meant a further scan of the units.

The Capey Review proposed a number of changes to GNVQ assessment intended to reduce the assessment burden and to increase the consistency of assessment. Many of these recommendations were then reinforced in the Dearing 16–19 Review, particularly the emphasis on increased external components to improve reliability.

Based on Capey's *GNVQ Assessment Review* (NCVQ 1995) recommendations, the revised GNVQ piloted from September 1997 incorporated the following changes:

▶ a move from element-based to unit-based assessment in which students undertake fewer and more in-depth assignments. The changed assumption here is that preparatory teaching and learning will take place and will not be assessed and recorded (at present much of this has to be assessed);

▶ simplified grading criteria: there will only be two grading themes and these will be 'contextualised' in each unit so the requirements are much more specific;

▶ a set assignment will be introduced for each GNVQ. This will be externally set, internally marked and externally moderated. It will meet all the requirements for the particular unit (i.e. students need *only* do this). The intention is to provide a standard task which will provide the basis for common marking standards;

▶ there will be fewer but more substantial tests, which will also contribute to grading (the tests are pass/fail only, at present). The purpose of these will be to test application of vocational knowledge and skills rather than the current 'coverage of range';

▶ key skills will be assessed both through set assignments and the portfolio;

▶ the current verification system will be modified so that students' work is sampled and centrally assessed. This is intended to improve the consistency of assessment.

As with NVQs, the changes to unit assessment and grading are similar to the national curriculum revision process, with its move from detailed Statements of Attainments to broad-based Level Descriptions. The increased 'externality' has echoes of coursework restrictions in GCSE and GCE. The assessment tension is to preserve the distinctiveness of GNVQ, with its emphasis on independent learning centred on coursework and applied knowledge, while meeting demands for more external components and more reliability in teacher assessment. This tension becomes more acute as parity with GCSE and GCE impacts on league tables (e.g. the GNVQ Part One Intermediate award counts as two A*–C GCSEs) and on Higher Education selection.

General and occupational pathways

Both NVQs and GNVQs are moving away from highly detailed coverage of criterion-referenced specifications, and more attention is being given to external components and reliability of the assessment regime. This raises the issues of what will happen to other vocational qualifications, currently outside Dearing's General and Vocational pathways, which wish to be nationally recognised (*'badged'*). What seems most likely is that there will be criteria within a pathway which any qualification will have to meet. These criteria are likely to be broadly parallel to those placed on GNVQs and NVQs in their respective pathways. This may mean similar weightings of external assessments and similar treatment of key skills.

This again raises the issues of how assessment regimes can best be developed to retain 'fitness-for-purpose' whilst providing sufficient rigour and reliability in the assessment. As we have seen with national curriculum and GCE/GCSE assessment, the pressure to ensure reliability may lead to an approach to assessment which may narrow the range of learning skills and reduce student motivation.

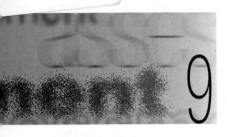

Conclusions: effective assessment

9

Throughout this book we have sought to tackle those assessment issues which impinge most directly on teachers and policy-makers. For many these are identified with national curriculum assessment and with examinations at 16 and 18, where the emphasis is on monitoring and comparing performance across schools, and on selection. However, we have also emphasised the importance of effective classroom assessment for learning.

Key issues

One of our recurrent themes has been the importance of being clear about the **purpose(s) of assessment**. In the first chapter we saw that, historically, assessment has been used for *selection*, by using examinations to assess an individual's ability or attainment rather than selecting on the basis of patronage. Questions may then be asked about the fairness of the examinations themselves, particularly if they disadvantage a particular group because of the content and assessment methods employed – issues of equity which we raised in chapter 5.

Another historical use of assessment has been to *raise standards*. We have explored the double-edged nature of using tests to do this: the nineteenth-century 'payment by results' illustrated the negative consequences of high-stakes assessment which equated learning to memorising what would be tested. We discussed in chapter 1 the complex issue of when testing merely leads to improvements in test scores and when, effectively linked to the curriculum, it genuinely improves learning.

The introduction of national performance tables in order to *monitor and compare the performance of institutions* has led to national curriculum assessment being used primarily for this evaluative purpose. This function places the emphasis on standardised testing and reliability, which in turn may begin to narrow both what is taught and the type of learning that is encouraged. There are also concerns about whether GCSE and GCE performance tables are encouraging schools to adopt examination entry strategies which benefit the schools' league table position rather than considering what is best for the individual student.

The emphasis on using assessment for accountability purposes, through mechanisms such as performance tables, has led to the relative neglect of another purpose: *assessment for learning*. Here assessment is used as part of the learning process, not as a summative check on what has been learned. The professional role of teachers is to use assessment as a means of helping students to learn. We have particularly emphasised the importance of feedback as a means of 'closing the gap' between actual performance and desired performance.

In looking at the development of the national curriculum it is clear that, as is usually the case, an attempt to serve multiple assessment purposes has come to grief, with the more formative and diagnostic uses the first casualties. As the main purpose becomes the monitoring and comparing of schools, so the emphasis is placed on external tests to ensure the reliability of these 'high-stakes' assessments. The teachers' role in the assessment is then diminished.

If we are clear about the purpose of an assessment then we need to find the most appropriate form of assessment to support that purpose – its **fitness-for-purpose**. A theme which has run throughout the book is that *assessment shapes both curriculum and teaching*. We saw in chapter 1 the distorting effects of the 'payment by results' scheme. In current examinations, what appears on past papers shapes how much of a syllabus is taught and what is emphasised. If a topic consistently appears on the examination paper, then students are likely to be prepared for it. Similarly, this mechanism has been used in national curriculum assessment to signal where teachers should concentrate their teaching. The introduction in 1997 of optional mental arithmetic tests at Key Stages 2 and 3, partly in response to concerns about unfavourable international comparisons, sends such a message. When the tests are compulsory, teachers will most certainly prepare pupils specifically for the test.

We argued in our section on Measurement Driven Instruction that the power of an assessment regime to determine curriculum and teaching is double-edged: at its best, it can improve the curriculum and make teaching more imaginative (e.g. the move from O level to GCSE), at its worst, it can reduce the curriculum to what is in the test and reduce teaching to training in test-taking techniques. George Madaus (1988) reminds us of Garrison Keillor's fictional example:

> ❛*For years, students of the senior class were required to read* [Phileopolis] *and answer questions about its meaning, etc. Teachers were not required to do so, but simply marked according to the correct answers supplied by Miss Quoist, including: (1) To extend the benefits of civilisation and religion to all peoples, (2) No, (3) Plato, and (4) A wilderness*

cannot satisfy the hunger for beauty and learning, once awakened. The test was the same from year to year, and once the seniors found the answers and passed them to the juniors, nobody read Philepolis *anymore.* **9**

(Garrison Keillor, *Lake Wobegon Days*)

We would cite Key Stage 2 national curriculum science as a successful balance of combining a compulsory science curriculum (where previously there had been little systematic science teaching) with testing and teacher assessment in a way which does not appear to have constrained teaching. The rapid improvement of English pupils' performances in the recent international science comparability study (see chapter 3) seems to bear this out.

In chapter 2 we dealt with the idea of **learning styles**, particularly the contrast between *deep* and *surface* learning. Deep-learning approaches emphasise learners actively thinking for themselves and organising their knowledge. Surface learning is more likely to involve accepting and reproducing content and ideas. The *strategic learner* is the student who mixes the two approaches to best effect: for example, rote learning for vocabulary and spelling; deep learning for integrating ideas. The issue in assessment is whether most of our tests and examinations encourage surface learning at the expense of deep learning. In a study by Ramsden *et al* (1987) university students were given training to improve learning skills, with the expectation that they would make more use of deep approaches. In reality, they found that the training led to an increase in surface learning as the students became better strategic learners – and realised that their course assessment procedures were best met by surface learning.

The form of assessment directly affects learning style. It seems obvious that if one of our aims is to produce flexible and innovative thinkers, then our assessment should call for imaginative responses. Crooks (1988) quotes distinguished university physics educator, E. M. Roberts:

6*Examinations tell them [the students] our real aims, at least so they believe. If we stress clear understanding and aim at growing knowledge of physics, we may completely sabotage our teaching by a final examination that asks for numbers to be put into memorised formulas. However loud our sermons, however intriguing the experiments, students will judge by that examination – and so will next year's students who hear about it.* **9**

(p.445)

We have emphasised the importance of assessment *for* learning, particularly as this is often eclipsed by the demands of summative assessment (*of* learning). In chapter 2 we explored ways in which teacher assessment can contribute to the learning process. Effective assessment helps:

- ▶ **motivate students to learn;**
- ▶ **students (and teachers) decide what to learn;**
- ▶ **students learn how to learn;**
- ▶ **students learn to judge the effectiveness of their learning.**

Of particular importance in this is the process of *feedback*. We have used this in the fairly narrow sense of information/activity which successfully *closes the gap* between what is intended (a standard that the student also recognises) and what is achieved. Assessment in which the gap is signalled but provides no means of closing it (e.g. *'a good effort* – 7/10') does not count as feedback under this definition, while guidance on the steps needed to improve performance would. Adopting this approach is demanding: it requires professional skill to identify what the next step is and requires honest appraisal of the performance. Sadler (1989) gives the example of *not* rewarding students who put a lot of effort into a piece of work but completely miss the point: to have rewarded them, he argues, would not help the student learn that the critical first step is to grasp what is expected.

One of the requirements for a scheme of assessment to be fit-for-purpose is that it needs to be *straightforward* enough for those who use it to be able to assess reliably and to make sense of the results. We saw in the early versions of national curriculum assessment that the criterion-referenced schemes were too complex and too detailed. The consequence was that the benefits of such detailed assessment were lost, as overloaded teachers made little use of the findings and had little confidence in the results. Similarly, vocational qualifications have suffered from over-detailed specification in which assessment is perceived as a fragmented and bureaucratic 'tickbox' activity (chapter 8). The definition of **validity** which broadens its meaning to include the use to which the results of a test are put is relevant here: if results are misunderstood or mis-used, validity is reduced.

There is a tension here, however, in that in the move to much simpler schemes of assessment we end up with limited information. We reported in chapter 4 how the early national curriculum SATs, despite their time-consuming demands, were subsequently seen as providing valuable diagnostic information. In contrast, the results from current tests do not seem to be used formatively, and quickly become what Patricia Broadfoot (1994) calls 'dead data'. In particular, sending key stage tests out to external markers means that teachers lose much valuable information when the tests are returned to the schools. The main use teachers appear to make of them is to check the marking to see whether there should be an appeal.

The task is therefore to develop schemes of assessment which are relatively simple to use, yet which provide useful information about the learning and attainments of the students. The treatment of **reliability** in chapter 4 can be linked to this. Reliability is seen there as part of the broader construct of **dependability** – an assessment should be judged on whether it has disclosed the real achievements of the student and whether this has been recorded effectively ('fidelity'). The assessment of many students under test conditions may not be reliable because their performance was depressed by the anxieties that test conditions generate.

It is also important that there be public credibility: test users and the general public need to be reassured that results are consistent and comparable. The early Key Stage 1 SATs fell foul of this criterion, as did coursework in the early days of GCSE.

A further consideration in any scheme of assessment is **utility** (Nuttall 1987): its manageability and cost-effectiveness. It is quite possible to devise an assessment instrument that would be seen as valid (because it samples from the whole domain using a variety of fit-for-purpose techniques) and reliable (because it offers students opportunities for optimal performance and the marking is highly consistent) yet which is both impractical and prohibitively expensive. Even the driving test, which most candidates regard as uncomfortably thorough, does not require night driving, motorway driving or driving in a variety of weather conditions. Important as these are, the utility arguments against sampling these are hardly likely to be challenged.

Our main concern in relation to utility is the *cost* of national curriculum testing. An assessment system which tests all pupils at ages 7, 11, 14 and 16 and which then publishes national performance tables is very expensive, particularly if the main use of the results is to provide school level averages of performance. We are not aware of another country which tests on this scale. In order to monitor national standards, most countries use *sampling* techniques which provide reliable 'low stakes' assessment. Even where schools are compared, this is done by using a sample of students who may take a variety of tests, but who are not individually identified ('matrix sampling'). Below we offer some suggestions on how to make better use of the resources currently going in to national testing.

Fairness has surfaced as a theme in a variety of forms throughout the book. We saw with selection that the intention was to make this *more* fair through the use of examinations. Similarly the development of IQ testing was to identify those who had special educational needs – though this then moved on, in the form of the eleven-plus examination, to identify those who would benefit from an academic (i.e. grammar school) education. Recent concerns have focused on the performance of boys and girls and the vexed issue of whether public examinations are unfair to one gender or whether the differences in pass rates and high scores reflect actual, and different, underlying levels of attainment.

Research on the performance of ethnic minority students has also highlighted the issue of fairness: as long as monitoring of different (potentially disadvantaged) groups' performance is not carried out on a regular basis, any inequalities will not be dealt with and group differences in performance will widen.

Improving assessment

Throughout this book we have raised a number of concerns about the uses to which assessments – especially national assessments – are being put. In particular, we are uneasy about the over-emphasis on the use of assessment to monitor performance, and the corresponding lack of priority on the use of classroom assessment as part of the learning process. In making suggestions about how we could strike a better balance, we acknowledge our debt to the BERA Assessment Task Group.

1 Re-focus national curriculum assessment

We think that the purpose of national curriculum assessment should be reviewed and that at different key stages we should consider different purposes.

KEY STAGE 1
The purpose of assessment at this stage should be formative, to give teachers a clear picture of the relative strengths and weaknesses of each pupil. Teachers could be provided with a selection of manageable tasks and tests (e.g. reading) which they would use. The results would not be put in national performance tables, and therefore the assessments could be made over a longer period of time (i.e. they do not have to be taken on the same day), possibly on an 'as ready' basis, as in Scotland; this would also take account of the very different levels of maturity and learning found between those just turning 7 and those turning 8. It would encourage assessment of a wider range of skills which could be reported to parents in the form of a profile. This profile would be brought up to date at the end of Key Stage 1 and provide the baseline for any value-added analysis at the end of primary school.

KEY STAGE 2
We recognise that assessment at 11 will be used mainly to evaluate the performance of schools as most pupils reach the end of the primary phase, though we do not see a need for national performance tables: comparisons should be at local level. We would wish to see more use made at transfer to secondary school of pupils' assessments at Key Stage 2. If we wished to monitor a broader range of attainment than the current testing allows, this could be done by APU-style sampling (see below).

KEY STAGE 3
The expensive tests and national performance tables for 14 year olds are difficult to justify. Pupils take the tests *after* they have selected their GCSE options. They will often have changed teachers and courses, so that results have little formative impact. Relative performance of schools at Key Stage 3

is easily overshadowed by their GCSE results. Any value-added approaches are likely to use performance at 11 as the baseline and at 16 as the 'output'.

We suggest that a more effective use of resources would be to sample national performance using APU-style techniques, which allow a much broader range of skills and knowledge to be assessed in a 'low stakes' setting and will provide information about what pupils – at, say, two stages of their national curriculum programme – have achieved. There is also a case for providing a battery of tasks which teachers can use as a basis for teacher assessment and which could be reported to parents. There are successful examples of this approach in Northern Ireland and Scotland. Once again this opens up the possibility of assessing Year 9 pupils as soon as they are ready to complete a level – an approach which also allows a more diagnostic use of the assessments.

2 Re-allocate resources

Testing nationally every pupil at 7, 11, 14 and 16 has led to an expensive and high-stakes assessment regime. As we saw in the first two chapters, testing in itself does not guarantee improved learning. Far more important to learning is effective teacher assessment. We would like to see far more resources allocated to the professional development of teachers' assessment skills and away from the current testing regime, to allow us to move closer to Sadler's requirements for effective teaching and learning through feedback. We believe that moderation meetings and agreement trials at a local level would do much to enhance these skills, together with the production of exemplar materials and of high-quality optional tasks for teachers.

3 Use value-added approaches effectively

We saw in chapter 3 that the unfairness of league tables based on raw results has led to the call for value-added approaches, which recognise the contribution that a school makes to a student's progress. The danger is, as David Reynolds has pointed out, that value-added is being treated as policy and an end-in-itself, rather than only as a tool and an instrument of policy. In other words, the value-added findings should be diagnostic and lead to action, rather than legitimating current standards within a school. The key problem here, Reynolds observes, is that *value-added, put simply, makes it possible for low levels of achievement to be regarded as a relatively successful outcome of a school*' (*TES*, 21 March 1997). We accept this point: even a school which has an impressive value-added rating (because pupils entered with minimal achievement) has not 'done its job' if pupils move on without the skills to cope with the next phase of education or with the demands of the workplace.

Will Hutton has made a similar case, pointing out that New Labour (pre-election) no longer aims for equality of outcome, preferring instead to work for equality of opportunity ('Here's a primary objective for New Labour', *Observer*, 16 March 1997). He argues that this is a misguided approach in relation to primary schooling, particularly the use of league tables, since we should not be content to see a wide variation of primary school performance. He argues that we must look for equality of outcome as the foundation for giving equality of opportunity for all school leavers, since progress in the primary phase is vital to later learning.

The consequence of this 'zero tolerance' line of reasoning is that there would be a shift of resources to introduce '*massive programmes of positive discrimination, of which two types are likely to be needed: that to most schools with disadvantaged intakes, and that to those schools that perform poorly despite having good intakes*' (Reynolds, *op cit*).

4 Encourage broader learning and assessment

We saw in chapter 2 that while our aim may be to produce 'active learners' who would be reflective about the way they learn, in practice our teaching and testing may over-emphasise 'surface learning'. We want to see an approach to assessment which encourages the 'strategic learner' to use a range of learning strategies combining 'surface' and 'deep' approaches in the process of assessing both basic and higher-order skills.

We believe there is a place for surface learning which uses techniques of repetition to embed basic knowledge. Our reflections on the standards achieved by Pacific Rim countries in maths and science (chapter 3) showed how important the emphasis on interactive learning is – in contrast to more Anglo-Saxon assumptions about traditional approaches to rote learning, which see it as a passive process.

It is important to place more emphasis on the pupil's own active learning. Timed tests are a poor vehicle for this and therefore we would like to see more emphasis on tasks and teacher assessment. Some of the earlier national curriculum standard assessment tasks (SATs), used on a voluntary basis, could contribute to more effective teaching and learning.

5 Offer a broader experience of learning and assessment in examinations

The role of public examinations in selection of students and in evaluation of schools and colleges makes them high-stakes qualifications. This, as we saw in chapters 3, 7 and 8, leads to an emphasis on reliability in their design and a pressure to use externally set and marked tests and examinations. This in turn limits the skills and knowledge that are taught and assessed. The recent reduction in coursework in both GCSE and GCE A level examinations, and the increased number of external components in the revised GNVQ, attest to this trend.

There has to be concern that students – particularly the most able who go on to A level – will go through the education system experiencing an increasingly narrow range of assessment styles. Tests at 7, 11 and 14, written examinations at 16 and 18, coupled with narrowing subject specialism from 16 to 18 years, are likely to lead to 'test-taking' learning styles and a restricted curriculum diet.

While Sir Ron Dearing's *Review of Qualifications for 16–19 Year Olds* sought to broaden this diet by encouraging the uptake of Key Skills and proposing a National Diploma across several 'areas of experience', the response from subject specialists and from course planners has been lukewarm. Anything less than this is seen as merely tinkering with the system by those who want a more radical and flexible approach to learning for the next century.

The future

It is important to encourage students to have a variety of learning and assessment experiences along the lines that we have described. Our current system may be narrowing this experience and we may have to look again at introducing more variety. This will include reconsidering the contribution of coursework and teacher assessment which, in the words of Henry Macintosh (1986), have fallen foul of *'the British obsession for preferring to do worse on those examinations which carry greater prestige rather than do better on those that are more useful'*.

With the information revolution gathering speed, we must accept that the students we are now assessing will be working in a very different environment: all information will be only six seconds away in the *'instantaneous, 24-hour information world'* (Dalin and Rust 1996). Thus, learning how to learn must become a fundamental aim of schooling. In taking a longer-term perspective on assessment, we raise four key issues.[3]

Emphasise the local rather than the global
The teacher must remain central to assessment, which itself is grounded in a 'local' context which allows flexibility of approach. Rigour can be maintained by reporting against national standards and using external moderation.

Emphasise the subjective rather than the objective
Putting the learner at the centre in assessment is critical. This means treating the learner more as a partner, and involves redefining power relations in assessment. This does not mean teachers giving up control, as our examples of constructive feedback with 7-year-old children showed

[3]This section draws on Caroline Gipps' inaugural lecture *Assessment for the millennium: form, function and feedback*, Institute of Education, University of London, 1996.

(chapter 2) – it means learners taking responsibility for their performance and monitoring their learning. We know both of these are vital to effective learning, and it is never too young to start.

Accept a range of assessment strategies

We have argued in chapter 5 that part of equity in assessment is to provide assessment strategies which give *all* learners a chance to perform well. The diversity among pupils as individuals and as learners supports this need for variety. What we know about differences among learners challenges any assessment regime that assumes that everyone can and does learn in the same way (Gardner 1991).

Advances in technology will lead to new options in assessment

The development of electronic networks (telephone, video, e-mail, etc) have a huge potential for assessment:

▶ **oral and practical examinations can be carried out from a distance (5 year olds are talking to each other in the Western Isles, so examiners should be able to);**

▶ **scripts can be marked and moderated without being posted – as scanners become as familiar as faxes;**

▶ **markers, moderators, test and examination developers can operate on the Internet.**

There are some very positive and creative ways in which the new technology can be used for assessment: going electronic does not have to mean going down the machine-administered and scored multiple-choice route.

As we have seen throughout the book, we already have sophisticated assessment practices which are capable of supporting learning and providing comparable and valid results. Central to these is effective assessment in the classroom, particularly in the years prior to selection and certification. We have also argued that the current focus on mass testing and reporting has placed too much emphasis on the purpose of evaluating schools, which in turn has narrowed assessment strategies. Life in the twenty-first century will call for more, rather than less, flexibility in our teaching, learning and assessments.

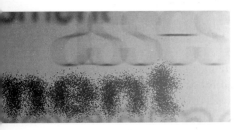

References

Airasian, P. (1988) 'Measurement driven instruction: a closer look', *Educational Measurement: Issues and Practice*, Winter, pp.6–11.

Apple, M. W. (1989) 'How equality has been redefined in the conservative restoration', in Secada, W. (ed.) *Equity and Education*, Falmer Press, New York.

Baker, E. and O'Neil, H. (1994) 'Performance assessment and equity: a view from the USA', *Assessment in Education*, *1*, 11–26.

Ball, S. (1990) *Politics and Policy Making in Education*, Routledge.

Bennett, S. N., Wragg, E. C., Carre, C. G. and Carter, D. S. G. (1991) 'A longitudinal study of primary teachers' perceived competence in, and concerns about, national curriculum implementation', *Research Papers in Education*, *7*, 1, 53–78.

Bibby, C. (1959) *T. H. Huxley: Scientist, Humanist and Educator*, Watts.

Black, P. (1993) 'The Shifting Scenery of the National Curriculum', in Chitty, C. and Simon, B. (eds) *Education Answers Back*, Lawrence and Wishart.

Bourdieu, P. and Passeron, J. C. (1977) *Reproduction in Education Society and Culture*, Sage Publications.

Broadfoot, P. (1979) *Assessment, Schools and Society*, Methuen.

Broadfoot, P. (1993) 'Performance assessment in perspective: Some international insights', paper presented at the AERA Conference, Atlanta.

Broadfoot, P. (1994) 'Diagnostic Discourse or Dead Data? Teacher Assessment at Key Stage 2', paper presented at the BERA annual conference, St Anne's College Oxford, 8–11 September 1994.

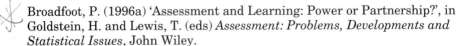
Broadfoot, P. (1996a) 'Assessment and Learning: Power or Partnership?', in Goldstein, H. and Lewis, T. (eds) *Assessment: Problems, Developments and Statistical Issues*, John Wiley.

Broadfoot, P. (1996b) *Education, Assessment and Society*, Open University Press.

Brown, M. (1988) 'Issues in formulating and Organising Attainment Targets on Relation to their Assessment', in *National Assessment and Testing: A Research Response*, edited by H. Torrance, BERA.

Brown, M., McCallum, B., Taggart, B. and Gipps, C. (1996) 'The validity of national testing at age 11: the teacher's view', submitted to *Assessment in Education*.

Burt, C. (1921) *Mental and Scholastic Tests*, Staples Press.

Carr-Saunders, A. M. and Wilson, P. A. (1933) *The Professions*, Oxford University Press.

Christie, T. and Forrest, G. M. (1981) *Defining Public Examination Standards*, Macmillan Educational.

Clarke, S. (1996) 'The impact of national curriculum statutory testing at Key Stages 1 and 2 on teaching and learning in the curriculum', *British Journal of Curriculum and Assessment*, 7, 1.

Claxton, G. (1995) 'What kind of learning does self-assessment drive? Developing a "nose" for quality: comments on Klenowski', *Assessment in Education*, 2, 339–43.

Cresswell, M. J. (1990) 'Gender effects in GCSE: some initial analyses', paper prepared for Nuffield Seminar, 29 June 1990, University of London, Institute of Education.

Cresswell, M. J.(1996) 'Defining, Setting and Maintaining Standards in Curriculum-embedded Examinations: Judgemental and Statistical Approaches', in Goldstein, H. and Lewis, T. (eds) *Assessment: Problems, Developments and Statistical Issues*, John Wiley.

Cresswell, M. J. and Houston, J. G. (1991) 'Assessment of the National Curriculum – some fundamental considerations', *Educational Review*, 43, 63–78.

Cronbach, L (1988) 'Five perspectives on validity argument', in Weiner, H. and Braun, H. (eds) *Test Validity*, Erlbaum, Princeton, NJ.

Crooks, T. J. (1988) 'The impact of classroom evaluation on students', *Review of Educational Research*, 5, 4, 438–81.

Dalin, P. and Rust, V. D. (1996) *Towards Schooling for the Twenty-First Century*, Cassell.

Daugherty, R. (1995) *National Curriculum Assessment: A review of policy 1987–1994*, Falmer Press.

Dearing, R. (1996) *Review of Qualifications for 16–19 Year Olds*, School Curriculum and Assessment Authority.

DES (1977) *Education in Schools: a consultative document*, HMSO.

DES (1985) *Better Schools*, HMSO.

DES (1987a) *The National Curriculum 5–16: a consultation document (TGAT Interim Report)*, DES/Welsh Office.

DES (1987b) *Improving the Basis For Awarding GCSE Grades*, unpublished paper, September 1987 (made available to TGAT).

DES (1988) *National Curriculum: Task Group on Assessment and Testing: A Report*, DES/Welsh Office.

Eckstein, M. A. (1996) 'A comparative assessment of assessment', *Assessment in Education*, 3, 2, 233–40.

Eggleston, J. (1984) 'School Examinations – Some Sociological Issues', in Broadfoot, P. (ed.) *Selection, Certification and Control*, Falmer Press.

Elwood, J. (1995) 'Undermining gender stereotypes: examination and coursework performance in the UK at 16', *Assessment in Education*, 2, 3, 283–303.

Elwood, J. and Comber, C. (1996) *Gender Differences in Examinations at 18+: Final Report*, Nuffield Foundation, Institute of Education.

Entwistle, N. (1992) *The Impact of Teaching in Learning Outcomes in Higher Education*, Sheffield CVCP Staff Development Unit.

EOC/Ofsted (1996) *The Gender Divide: Performance differences between boys and girls at school*, Equal Opportunities Commission and Office for Standards in Education.

Gardner, H. (1991) *The Unschooled Mind. How Children Think and How Schools Should Teach*, Fontana Press.

Gillborn, D. and Gipps, C. (1996) *Recent Research on the Achievements of Ethnic Minority Pupils*, Office for Standards in Education.

Gipps, C. (ed.) (1992) *Developing Assessment for the National Curriculum*, Bedford Way Series, ULIE/Kogan Page.

Gipps, C. (1994) *Beyond Testing: Towards a Theory of Educational Assessment*, Falmer Press.

Gipps, C. (1995) 'What do we mean by equity in relation to assessment?', *Assessment in Education*, 2, 3, 271–81.

Gipps, C. (1997) *Assessment in Primary Schools*, Curriculum Association.

Gipps, C., Brown, M., McCallum, B. and McAlister, S. (1995) *Intuition or Evidence? Teachers and National Assessment of Seven Year Olds*, Open University Press.

Gipps, C. and Goldstein, H. (1983) *Monitoring Children: An Evaluation of the Assessment of Performance Unit*, Heinemann Educational Books.

Gipps, C. V., McCallum, B., McAlister, S. and Brown, M. (1992) 'National Assessment at Seven: some emerging themes', in Gipps, C. V. (ed), *Developing Assessment for the National Curriculum*, Bedford Way Series, ULIE/Kogan Page.

Gipps, C. and Murphy, P. (1994) *A Fair Test? Assessment, Achievement and Equity*, Open University Press.

Gipps, C., Steadman, S., Blackstone, T. and Stierer, B. (1983) *Testing Children: Standardised Testing in Schools and LEAs*, Heinemann Educational Books.

Glaser, R. (1963) 'Instructional technology and the measurement of learning outcomes: Some questions', *American Psychologist*, 18, 519–21.

Goldstein, H. (1987) *Multilevel Models in Educational and Social Research*, Charles Griffin and Co.

Goldstein, H. (1993) 'Assessing group differences', *Oxford Review of Education*, 19, 141–50.

Goldstein, H. (1996) 'Group Differences and Bias in Assessment', in Goldstein, H. and Lewis, T. (eds) *Assessment: Problems, Developments and Statistical Issues*, John Wiley.

Goldstein, H., Thomas, S., O'Donoghue, C. and Knight, T. (1997) *DfEE Study of Value Added for 16–18 year olds in England*, DFEE.

Goldstein, H. and Woodhouse, G. (1988) *Educational Performance Indicators and LEA League Tables*, University of London, Institute of Education.

Goleman, D.(1995) *Emotional Intelligence*, Bloomsbury

Good, F. and Cresswell, M. (1988) *Grading the GCSE*, London: SEC.

Gray, J. (1996) 'The Use of Assessment to Compare Institutions', in Goldstein, H. and Lewis, T. (eds) *Assessment: Problems, Developments and Statistical Issues*, John Wiley.

Guskey, T. R. and Kifer, E. W. (1989) 'Ranking School Districts on the basis of Statewide Test Results: Is it meaningful or misleading?', paper presented at AERA Conference, San Francisco, March 1989.

Harlen, W. and James, M. (1997 in press) 'Assessment and learning: differences and relationships between formative and summative assessment', *Assessment in Education*.

HMI (1989) *The Introduction of the GCSE in schools 1986–88*, HMSO.

Holmes, E. (1911) *What Is and What Might Be*, Constable and Co.

House, E. (1978) 'An American view of British Accountability', in Becher, T. and Maclure, S. (eds) *Accountability in Education*, NFER.

IGRC (1992) *Differentiation in GCSE Mathematics: Centres' Entry Decision-making Policy*, University of Cambridge Local Examinations Syndicate.

JCTP (1988) *Code of Fair Testing Practices in Education*, Joint Committee on Testing Practices in Education, American Psychological Association, Washington DC.

Kellaghan, T. (1996) 'IEA studies and educational policy', *Assessment in Education*, *3*, 2, 143–60.

Kingdon, M. and Stobart, G. (1988) *GCSE Examined*, Falmer Press.

Klenowski, V. (1995) 'Student self-evaluation processes in student-centred teaching and learning contexts of Australia and England', *Assessment in Education*, *2*, 2, 145–85.

Klenowski, V. (1996) 'Connecting Assessment and Learning: Portfolio Assessment', IAEA Conference, Beijing.

Linn, M. C. (1992) Gender differences in educational achievement, *Sex Equity In Educational Opportunity, Achievement and Testing*, Educational Testing Service, Princeton, NJ.

Linn, R. L. (1993) 'Educational assessment: expanded expectations and challenges', *Educational Evaluation and Policy Analysis*, *15*, 1–16.

Macintosh, H. (1986) 'Sacred Cows of Coursework', in Gipps, C. (ed.) *The GCSE: An Uncommon Exam*, Bedford Way Papers, No. 29, University of London Institute of Education.

Mackintosh, N. J. and Mascie-Taylor, C. (1985) 'The IQ Question', *Annex D, The Swann Report, Education for All*, HMSO.

Madaus, G. (1988) 'The Influence of Testing on the Curriculum', in Tanner, L. (ed.), *Critical Issues in Curriculum, 87th Yearbook of NSSE Part 1*, University of Chicago Press, Chicago, Il., pp.83–121.

Madaus, G. (1992) 'A technological and historical consideration of equity issues associated with proposals to change the nation's testing policy', Symposium on Equity and Educational Testing and Assessment, Washington DC.

Marton, F. and Saljo, R. (1984) 'Approaches to Learning', in Marton, F., Hounsell, D. and Entwistle, N. (eds) *The Experience of Learning*, Scottish Academic Press.

Massey, A. J. (1995) 'Criterion-related test development and national test standards', *Assessment in Education*, 2, 2, 187–203.

McCallum, B. (1996) 'The transfer and use of assessment information between primary and secondary schools', *British Journal of Curriculum and Assessment*, 6, 3, 10–14.

Messick, S. (1989) 'Validity', in Linn, R. (Ed) *Educational Measurement* (3rd edn) American Council on Education, Washington, Macmillan.

Mislevy, R. J. (1993) 'Testing theory reconceived', paper presented at the NCME conference, Atlanta, April.

Mortimore, P., Sammons, P. and Thomas, S. (1994) 'School effectiveness and value-added measures', *Assessment in Education*, 1, 3, 315–32.

Murphy, P. (1990) 'Gender differences – implications for assessment and curriculum planning', paper presented to BERA conference, Roehampton, August.

Murphy, P. (1995) 'Assessment-Gender Implications', in Farrelly, D. (ed.) *Examinations in the Context of Change*, University College, Dublin.

Murphy, P. and Gipps, C. (Eds) (1996) *Equity in the Classroom. Towards Effective Pedagogy for Girls and Boys*, Falmer Press.

National Forum on Assessment (1992) 'Criteria for evaluation of student assessment systems', *Educational Measurement: issues and practice*, Spring.

NCVQ (1995) *GNVQ Assessment Review*, National Council for Vocational Qualifications.

Neave, G. (1988) 'Education and social policy: demise of an ethic or change of values?', *Oxford Review of Education*, 14, 3, 273–83.

Nuttall, D. (1987) 'The validity of assessments', *European Journal of Psychology of Education*, 11, 2, 108–18.

Nuttall, D. (1993), 'The ten-level scale', paper presented at the Conference of the Centre for Policy Studies, 21 September, ISEIC Institute of Education, University of London.

Nuttall, D. (1995) 'Problems in the Measurement of Change', in Murphy, R. and Broadfoot, P. (eds) *A Tribute to Desmond Nuttall*, Falmer Press.

Nuttall, D., Goldstein, H., Prosser, R. and Rasbash, H. (1989) 'Differential school effectiveness', *International Journal of Education Research*, 13, 769–76.

Ofsted/SCAA (1996) *Standards in Public Examinations 1975 to 1995*, Stationery Office.

Orr, R. and Nuttall, D. (1983) *Determining Standards in the proposed System of Examining at 16 plus*, Comparability in Examinations, Occasional Paper 2, London: Schools Council.

Pollard, A., Broadfoot, P., Croll, P., Osborn, M. and Abbott, D. (1994) *Changing English Primary Schools? The Impact of the Education Reform Act at Key Stage 1*, Cassell.

Ramsden, P., Beswick, D. and Bowden, J. (1987). 'Learning Processes and Learning Skills', in Richardson, J. T. E., Eysenck, M.W. and Piper, D.W. (eds) *Student learning: Research in education and cognitive psychology*, Open University Press.

Reynolds, D. and Farrell, S. (1996) *Worlds Apart? A Review of International Surveys of Educational Achievement involving England*, HMSO.

Sadler, R. (1989) 'Formative assessment and the design of instructional systems', *Instructional Science*, *18*, 119–44 .

Satterly, D. (1994) 'The Quality of External Assessment', in Harlen, W. (ed) *Enhancing Quality in Assessment*, Paul Chapman Publishers.

SCAA (1996) *Baseline Assessment Draft Proposals*, SCAA Com /96/556.

SEAC (1991) *National Curriculum Assessment at Key Stage 3: a review of the 1991 pilots with implications for 1992*, School Examinations and Assessment Council.

SEC (1984) *The Development of Grade-Related Criteria for the GCSE. A briefing paper for working parties*, Secondary Examinations Council.

Secondary School Examinations Council (1960) *The General Certificate of Education and Sixth Form Studies* (Third Report), HMSO.

Shepard, L. (1991) 'Psychometricians' beliefs about learning', *Education Researcher*, *20*, 7.

Shepard, L. (1992) 'What policy makers who mandate tests should know about the new psychology of intellectual ability and learning', in Gifford, B. and O'Connor, M. (eds) *Changing Assessments: Alternative Views of Aptitude, Achievement and Instruction*, Kluwer Academic Publishers.

Shorrocks, D., Daniels, S., Frobisher, L., Nelson, N., Waterson, A. and Bell, J. (1992) *ENCA 1 Project Report*, School Examinations and Assessment Council.

Smith, P. and Whetton, C. (1988) 'Bias reduction in test development', *The Psychologist*, July, pp.257–8.

Smithers, A. (1993) 'All Our Futures: Britain's Educational Revolution', *Dispatches Report on Education*, Channel Four Television.

Spearman, C. (1927) *The Ability of Man*, Macmillan.

Stobart, G. (1991) 'GCSE meets Key Stage 4: something had to give', *Cambridge Journal of Education*, *21*, 2, 177–87.

Stobart, G., Elwood, J. and Quinlan, M. (1992) 'Gender bias in examinations: how equal are the opportunities?', *British Educational Research Journal*, *118*, 3, 261–76.

Stobart, G., White, J., Elwood, J., Hayden, M. and Mason, K. (1992) *Differential Performance in Examinations at 16+: English and Mathematics*, School Examinations and Assessment Council.

Sutherland, G (1990) 'Education', in Thompson, F. M. L. (ed.) *The Cambridge Social History of Britain 1750–1950*, vol iii, Cambridge University Press.

Sutherland, G (1996) 'Assessment: Some Historical Perspectives', in Goldstein, H. and Lewis, T. (eds) *Assessment: Problems, Developments and Statistical Issues*, John Wiley.

Sutherland, G. (1984) *Ability, Merit and Measurement: Mental testing and English education, 1880–1940*, Oxford University Press.

Swann, M. (1985) *Education for All*, HMSO.

Thomson, G. O. B. and Sharp, S. (1988) 'History of Mental Testing', in Keeves, J. (ed.) *Educational Research Methodology and Measurement: An International Handbook*, Pergamon.

Torrance, H. (1993) 'Formative assessment: some theoretical problems and empirical questions', *Cambridge Journal of Education*, 23, 333–43.

Townshend, J. (1996) 'Comparing Performance Standards in Education', in Boyle, B. and Christie, T. (eds) *Issues in Setting Standards*, Falmer Press.

Tunstall, P. and Gipps, C. (1996a) 'How does your teacher help you make your work better?' Children's understanding of formative assessment', *The Curriculum Journal*, 7, 2, 185–203.

Tunstall, P. and Gipps, C. (1996b) 'Teacher feedback to young children in formative assessment: a typology', *British Educational Research Journal*, 22, 4, 389–404.

Weiss, J. (1987) 'The Golden Rule bias reduction principle: a practical reform', *Educational Measurement: Issues and Practice*, 6, no. 2, Summer 1987.

Wiliam, D. (1992) 'Some technical issues in assessment: a user's guide', *British Journal of Curriculum and Assessment*, 2, 3, 11–20.

Wiliam, D. (1996) 'Standard-setting Methods for Multiple Levels of Competence', in Boyle, B. and Christie, T. (eds) *Issues in Setting Standards*, Falmer Press.

Wiliam, D. and Black, P. (1996) 'Meanings and consequences: a basis for distinguishing formative and summative functions of assessment', *British Educational Research Journal*, 22, 5, 537–48.

Willis, D. (1992) 'Learning and Assessment: Exposing the inconsistencies of theory and practice', paper presented at University of London, Institute of Education.

Wilmut, J., Wood, R. and Murphy, R. J. L. (1996) *A Review of Research Into the Reliability of Examinations*, report prepared for SCAA.

Wolf, A. (1995) *Competence-based Assessment*, Open University Press.

Wood, R. (1985) *Testing*, Unit 21, E206, Block 4, Personality, Development and Learning, Open University.

Wood, R. (1986) 'The Agenda for Educational Measurement', in Nuttall, D. L. (ed.) *Assessing Educational Achievement*, Falmer Press.

Wood, R. (1987) 'Assessment and Equal Opportunities', public lecture at University of London, Institute of Education, 11 November 1987.

Wood, R. (1991) *Assessment and Testing. A Survey of Research*, Cambridge University Press.

Yates, L., (1985) 'Is "girl friendly schooling" really what girls need?', in Whyte, J., Deem, R., Kant, L. and Cruickshank, M. (eds) *Girl Friendly Schooling*, Methuen.

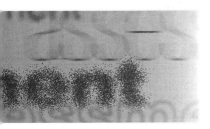

Subject Index